9.38

Lamontagne

¿El inglés? ¡Sin problemas!

Common problems in English for Spanish speakers – a dictionary and a guide

¿El inglés? ¡Sin problemas!

Common problems in English for Spanish speakers – a dictionary and a guide

MIKE O'NEILL

Nelson

Thomas Nelson and Sons Ltd
Nelson House Mayfield Road
Walton-on-Thames Surrey
KT12 5PL UK

51 York Place
Edinburgh
EH1 3JD UK

Thomas Nelson (Hong Kong) Ltd
Toppan Building 10/F
22A Westlands Road
Quarry Bay Hong Kong

First published by Edward Arnold

ISBN 0-340-51023-4

This edition first published by Thomas Nelson and Sons Ltd 1991

ISBN 0-17-556-081-1
NPN 9 8 7 6 5 4 3 2

Printed in Hong Kong

Introduction

This book is intended for Spanish-speaking students of English, of whatever level. It is basically an 'information bank' of the most common errors and problems encountered by students, whether the result of 'interference' from Spanish, or simply a difficulty caused by the internal structure of English.

It can be used in class by students following a formal English course, by autonomous learners at home, or by anyone who uses English in their work or studies. In addition to being a reference book, it can also be used to improve the student's language skills, particularly in writing (composition work etc.). Students can use it throughout a language course, from one level to another.

With autonomous learners particularly in mind, the structure of the book has been kept extremely simple. Items are listed alphabetically, without regard to their grammatical function; a detailed knowledge of grammatical terms is therefore not required to find any given reference. (In my experience, this is one of the main problems encountered by students - and even teachers! - when faced with trying to find an item in one of the many detailed grammar reference books available.)

Under each item heading there is a brief explanation, in English, of the problem; underneath, on the left, is the correct Spanish sentence where the difficulty arises; on the right, first of all an incorrect example in English, clearly marked as wrong, and then, below it, the correct version. If the problem is one of vocabulary, i.e. an English word which is often wrongly used by Spanish speakers (e.g. sensible, impressive etc.), a correct use of that word is also given. See the example given below.

Plenty (of)

(explanation of the problem):
Plenty (of) expresses quantity and is used with uncountable or plural nouns. It can not be used as an adjective to describe e.g. a room or a bus, etc. which contain a large number of people: for this, we use *full* or *crowded*.

(correct Spanish sentence):
La playa estaba llena.

(incorrect English sentence*):
⊗The beach was plenty of people.⊗

(correct English sentence):
The beach was FULL of people.
(or: The beach was CROWDED.)

(correct Spanish sentence):
Tenemos pan y queso de sobra pero necesitamos más mantequilla.

(correct use of *plenty*):
We have PLENTY of bread and cheese but we need more butter.

*The symbol ⊗ at the beginning and end of a sentence indicates that this sentence is incorrect English.

The items are ordered alphabetically in English in the text and there is a comprehensive index in Spanish (although English items such as *Ago* and *Word order* are also included), in order to allow the student to find relevant information in two separate ways. Please note that it is not an index to every Spanish word used in the text, but rather to Spanish words or expressions which students have problems translating and/or using correctly in English, e.g. 'bastante', 'esperar', 'puede que . . .' etc. Items such as 'animales', 'cerrar' and 'película' do not, therefore, appear in the index.

Acknowledgements

I should like to thank Mireia Bosch of the Escola Oficial d'Idiomes, Barcelona, and Lourdes Gracia for their help in correcting and improving the Spanish text; and above all, my colleague John McDowell at the British Council Institute, Barcelona for his invaluable advice, suggestions and encouragement, which made this book possible.

A

A(N) (Indefinite article) See also ONE.

(1) It must be used with professions.

Mi padre es profesor. ⊗My father is teacher.⊗
My father is A teacher.

(2) It cannot be used before an uncountable or plural noun.

Teníamos buen tiempo. ⊗We had a nice weather.⊗
We had NICE weather.

Lleva un pantalón nuevo. ⊗He's wearing a new trousers.⊗
He's wearing NEW trousers.

Actual(ly)

This means *real(ly)*, *in fact*, and is normally used for emphasis. To translate 'actual (mente)', we must use *currently*, *at the moment*, *nowadays* etc.

Actualmente, la situación económica se encuentra en un estado muy grave. ⊗Actually, the economy is in a terrible state.⊗
AT THE MOMENT, the economy is in a terrible state.
(or: The economy is CURRENTLY in a terrible state.)

Actualmente, el paro es un gran problema. ⊗Unemployment is a very actual problem.⊗
Unemployment is a big problem NOWADAYS.

–¿Eres de Londres, no?
–No, no, soy de Bath.
"You're from London, aren't you?".
"No, I'm from Bath, ACTUALLY."

Adjectives

There are five common mistakes with adjectives.

(1) Position: they must come before the noun in English.

Es una obra muy interesante. ⊗It's a play very interesting.⊗
It's a very INTERESTING play.

(2) Plurals: adjectives have no plural form.

Ambas películas eran emocionantes. ⊗Both films were excitings.⊗
Both films were EXCITING.

(3) Related to (2): certain adjectives are used with the definite article to refer to groups of people, but again, there is no plural form.

La ONCE es una organización para los ciegos.	⊗O.N.C.E. is an organisation for the blinds.⊗ O.N.C.E. is an organisation for the BLIND.

(4) There is a series of adjectives which are often confused, e.g. bored and boring. The '-ed' adjectives refer to states or feelings (e.g. 'estar aburrido'); the '-ing' adjectives refer to qualities of e.g. a film or a book (e.g. 'ser aburrido'). Some of the most common adjectives with these two forms are: *embarrassed, excited, interested, surprised, tired.*

El viaje fue muy cansado.	⊗The journey was very tired.⊗ The journey was very TIRING.
Está muy aburrida: no tiene nada que hacer.	⊗She is very boring: she has nothing to do.⊗ She is very BORED: she has nothing to do.

(5) Comparative and superlative forms – see MORE and MOST.

Adverbs

The most common general error with adverbs is using them with verbs of perception, e.g. to look, to feel, to smell, to sound, to seem, where an adjective should be used, because it is the subject, and not the action, which is being described.

Ese vestido le sienta muy bien.	⊗She looks well in that dress.⊗ She looks NICE/GOOD in that dress.
¡ Mmm! ¡ Huele muy bien!	⊗Mmm! That smells fantastically!⊗ Mmm! That smells FANTASTIC!

Advice

Advice is uncountable; we give someone *(some) advice* or *a piece of advice* but not *an advice* or *advices*.

¿Me puedes dar un consejo?	⊗Can you give me an advice?⊗ Can you give me SOME advice?
Mis padres siempre me dieron buenos consejos.	⊗My parents always gave me good advices.⊗ My parents always gave me good ADVICE.

Afraid

The expression *I'm afraid* literally means 'tengo miedo' but it is often used to mean *I'm sorry, but . . .*, to introduce bad news, a polite refusal, etc. It is not used with 'but'.

Lo siento, no está en casa.	⊗I'm afraid, but he's not at home.⊗ I'm afraid HE'S not at home. (or: I'm sorry, BUT he's not at home.)

After See also BEFORE, WHEN

There are 3 principal errors made with *after*.

(1) *After* is not normally used as an adverb; instead, we use *afterwards* or *after that* or *later* or *and then*.

Comimos, y después fuimos a pasear.	⊗We had lunch, and after, went for a walk.⊗ We had lunch and THEN/AFTER THAT/AFTERWARDS/LATER went for a walk.

(2) It is never used with the infinitive of a verb, but with the '–ing' form or with the predicate (full subject and verb).

Después de cerrar la puerta se sentó.	⊗After to close the door, he sat down.⊗ After CLOSING the door, (After HE CLOSED the door) he sat down.

(3) It is not used with the future tense, but with the present or present perfect, even when there is a future meaning.

Llámame cuando llegues.	⊗Ring me after you will arrive.⊗ Ring me after you ARRIVE.

Age

(1) The verb used for age is *to be*, not *to have*.

Él tiene 25 años.	⊗He has 25(years).⊗ He IS 25.

(2) After a number we can say *years old* but not *years* only.

Ella tiene 30 años.	⊗She is 30 years.⊗ She is 30 YEARS OLD.

(3) To ask someone their age, we say *How old are you?* and not a question with *years*.

¿Cuántos años tienes?	⊗How many years have you?⊗ HOW OLD ARE YOU?

Ago

(1) It is only used with the Past tense, not the Present Perfect.

Vi la película hace 3 semanas.	⊗I have seen the film 3 weeks ago.⊗ I SAW the film 3 weeks ago.

(2) It comes after, not before, an expression of time.

Hace 6 años vivía allí.	He lived there 6 years AGO.

To agree

(1) It cannot be used with *to be*.

Estoy de acuerdo contigo.	⊗I am agree with you.⊗
	I AGREE with you.
No estamos de acuerdo.	⊗We are not agree.⊗
	We DON'T agree.

(2) It can be followed by a verb in the infinitive but not in the '-ing' form.

Acordaron enviarle dinero.	⊗They agreed sending her some money.⊗
	They agreed TO SEND her some money.

All

(1) *All* is not normally used on its own to mean *everything*: it is nearly always used with a relative clause.

Me lo contó todo.	⊗She told me all.⊗
	She told me EVERYTHING. (She told me ALL SHE KNEW).

(2)a) *All* and *every* are similar but not identical. *All* is used, without *the*, with a plural noun and verb; *every* with a singular noun, when speaking about people or things in general.

Todos los animales tienen instinto de supervivencia.	⊗All the animals have a survival instinct.⊗
	ALL ANIMALS HAVE (EVERY ANIMAL HAS) a survival instinct.

b) *All* can be used with a singular to mean *the whole(of)*; *every* cannot be used in this way.

Trabaja todo el día.	⊗He works every day.⊗ (see 2c)
	He works ALL DAY.

c) We do not use *all (the)* . . . and a plural noun in expressions talking about habitual or repeated actions; instead, we use *every* with a singular noun.

Todos los martes, tenemos clase de Literatura.	⊗All the Tuesdays we have a Literature class.⊗
	EVERY TUESDAY we have a Literature class.

Almost See HARDLY

Alone

This word is often confused with *lonely* and *only*. *Alone* usually has the meaning of *not with other people*; *lonely* is a feeling of needing company (for people) or being isolated (for places); *only* usually has the sense of 'únicamente' or 'no más de'.

Lo hizo él solo.	⊗He did it only.⊗
	He did it ALONE/ON HIS OWN.
Tienen pocos amigos; se sienten muy solos.	⊗They are alone people; they have few friends.⊗
	They are LONELY people; they have few friends.

Es un pueblo aislado en la montaña.	It's a LONELY village in the mountains.
¡Compre ahora! ¡Sólo 500 ptas.!	Buy now! ONLY £2.50!
Solamente había 5 o 6 personas en el cine.	There were ONLY 5 or 6 people in the cinema.

Already See also STILL

(1) *Already* is often confused with *still* and *yet*. *Already* is used to talk about an action which has taken place earlier or more quickly than expected. *Yet* is normally used in negative or interrogative sentences for something that is or was expected to happen. *Still* is used when an action continues (often when we would expect it to have finished).

Aún no he acabado el informe.	⊗I haven't finished the report already.⊗ I haven't finished the report YET.
¿Ya has terminado ese trabajo?	Have you done that work ALREADY? (expressing surprise)
¿Has hecho ese trabajo?	Have you done that work YET? (simply asking a yes/no question)
Sólo lleva 3 meses trabajando allí y ya lo han ascendido.	⊗He's only been working there for 3 months and he's been promoted yet.⊗ He's only been working there for 3 months and he's been promoted ALREADY. (expressing surprise)
Los científicos todavía buscan un remedio para el cáncer.	⊗Scientists are already looking for a cure for cancer.⊗ Scientists are STILL looking for a cure for cancer. (It has been a problem for a long time)

(2) When *already* is used to speak about whether an action has happened, we normally use the Present Perfect in British English (in American English, the Simple Past is used).

Ya he visto esa película.	⊗I already saw that film.⊗ I'VE ALEADY SEEN that film.

Although See THOUGH

Always See EVER

Among See BETWEEN

Amusing

Amusing has a similar meaning to *funny* in the sense of *comic*, something which makes you laugh. Something which does not make you laugh or smile can be *enjoyable* or *entertaining* but not *amusing*. (See also FUNNY)

La visita al museo fue muy interesante – vimos muchos objetos romanos antiguos.	⊗The museum visit was very amusing – we saw a lot of old Roman objects.⊗

	The museum visit was very ENJOYABLE/INTERESTING – we saw a lot of old Roman objects.
Contó muchos chistes divertidos.	He told a lot of AMUSING jokes.

And

(1) *And* is used to connect 2 things or parts of a sentence when there is no contrast. If there is contrast, we must use *but*.

Fui a la estación a toda prisa pero ya había salido el tren.	⊗I rushed to the station and the train had already gone.⊗ I rushed to the station BUT the train had already gone.

(2) When 2 or more adjectives come before a noun in a sentence, we do not usually join them with *and* unless they are of the same kind (e.g. 2 colours, 2 words describing someone's character etc.).

Era un edificio grande y blanco.	⊗It was a big and white building.⊗ It was a big, white building.
Es un viejo muy aburrido.	⊗He's a boring and old man.⊗ He's a boring old man.
Es una persona afectuosa y simpática.	She's a warm (AND) friendly person.

Another

Another is followed by a singular noun except when there is a *number* or *a few* with a plural noun – see OTHER for full details.

Lo explicó a John y a otros amigos.	⊗He told John and another friends about it.⊗ He told John and OTHER friends about it.

Any See also SOME

(1) *Any* cannot be used before a singular, countable noun (we use *a* or *an*).

No tengo libro(s).	⊗I haven't got any book.⊗ I haven't got A book. (I haven't got ANY books).
¿Has visto alguna película buena últimamente?	⊗Have you seen any good film recently?⊗ Have you seen ANY good FILMS (A good FILM) recently?

(2) It is normally used in place of *some* in questions (and negative sentences) but not when we expect the answer *Yes*.

(in a shop) *¿Tienen plátanos?*	Have you got ANY bananas?
(in a house) *¿Te apetece un té?*	⊗Would you like any tea?⊗ Would you like SOME tea?

¿Me pone un poco de carne?	⊗Could I have any meat, please?⊗
	Could I have SOME meat, please?

(3) It cannot be used with a negative meaning unless accompanied by *not*.

–¿Alguna pregunta?	"Any questions/problems?"
–¿Algún problema?	⊗"Any questions/problems."⊗
–Ninguna/ninguno.	"(No), NO questions/problems."
	("No, NONE.")

(4) Notice that *any* can also have the meaning of 'cualquier' in the affirmative.

Escoge el libro que quieras.	Choose ANY book you like.

Anybody/anyone

See also ANY, ANYONE

These words have exactly the same meaning.

(1) In the affirmative, they mean 'cualquiera'.

Cualquiera puede aprender un idioma extranjero.	ANYONE/ANYBODY can learn a foreign language.

(2) In an interrogative expression, they normally replace *somebody/someone*.

–¿Conoces a alguien del pueblo?	⊗"Do you know somebody in the village?"⊗
	"Do you know ANYBODY in the village?"

(3) They only have a negative meaning when used with a negative verb – if the verb is affirmative, we use *nobody/no one*.

–Conoces a alguien del pueblo?	"Do you know anybody in the village?"
–No, a nadie.	⊗"No, anyone/anybody."⊗
	"No, NO ONE/NOBODY."
No había nadie en la calle.	⊗There was anyone in the street.⊗
	There was NOBODY/NO ONE in the street. (There WASN'T ANYBODY/ANYONE in the street.)

Anyone

There is an additional problem with *anyone*.

(1) It is sometimes confused with *any one*, which means *whichever one you want/like*.

–¿Qué libro puedo coger?	"Which book can I take?"
–Coge el que quieras.	⊗"Take anyone you like."⊗
	"Take ANY ONE you like."
¿Encontraste a alguien?	Did you meet ANYONE?

(2) *Any one* cannot be used in a negative sense when answering a question.

–¿Tienes discos?	"Have you got any records?"
– No, ninguno.	⊗"Any one."⊗
	"(No), NONE."
	("No, I HAVEN'T GOT ANY.")

Anything

Anything cannot have a negative meaning when used on its own: it acquires a negative meaning when used with a negative verb. (See also ANY and ANYBODY.)

No pasaba nada.	⊗Anything was happening.⊗ NOTHING was happening.
No veía nada.	I couldn't see ANYTHING.

Appointment

This means 'una cita' but only in a formal sense – e.g. a business appointment, or to see the doctor/dentist. For a boy meeting a girl socially, we say *to have a date* or simply *to meet*.

Ayer llamé a Mary y quedamos para mañana a las 8.	⊗I rang Mary yesterday and we made an appointment for 8.00 tomorrow.⊗ I rang Mary yesterday and we made a DATE for 8.00 tomorrow. (I'M MEETING HER at 8.00. . . .)
Acabo de llamar al dentista para pedir hora.	I've just made an APPOINTMENT to see the dentist.

To arrive

This verb is never followed by *to*; it is used with *in* for cities, towns and countries, and with *at* for specific places or buildings in a town or city.

Llegaron a Londres la semana pasada.	⊗They arrived to London last week.⊗ They arrived IN London last week.
Llegó al cine/teatro/a casa de Paul/a su despacho a las 8.	⊗She arrived to/in the cinema/theatre/Paul's house/her office at 8 o'clock.⊗ She arrived AT the cinema/AT the theatre/AT Paul's house/AT her office at 8 o'clock.

As   See LIKE, HOW

To ask

(1) We don't use *to* before the person who is asked.

Se lo preguntaré a Peter.	⊗I will ask to Peter.⊗ I will ASK PETER.

(2) If *to ask* has 2 objects, the person is placed first.

Pídele la hora a ese señor.	⊗Ask the time to that man.⊗ ASK THAT MAN THE TIME.

(3) We normally use *for* after *to ask* when the object is something given but not when it is something a person tells you.

Les pidió su ayuda.	⊗She asked their help.⊗ She asked FOR their help.
Preguntó cómo se llamaba la calle.	⊗He asked for the name of the street.⊗ He asked THE NAME of the street.

(4) In indirect requests, we say *to ask to do* something, not *to ask that* someone. . . . .

Les pidió que le esperasen.	⊗He asked that they waited for him.⊗ He asked THEM TO WAIT for him.

To assist

To assist means *to help*. To translate 'asistir', we say *to attend* or *to go to*.

El sábado pasado asistí a una boda.	⊗I assisted at/to a wedding last Saturday.⊗ I WENT TO/ATTENDED a wedding last Saturday.
No me queda dinero. ¿Me puedes ayudar?	I have no money left: can you ASSIST/HELP me?

To avoid

(1) You *avoid* a situation when that situation already exists. You *prevent* something which has not happened yet.

La ONU es una organización que intenta impedir que haya guerras.	⊗The U.N. is an organisation which tries to avoid war.⊗ The U.N. is an organisation which tries to PREVENT war.
Salió a las 6 de la madrugada para evitar la hora punta.	He left at 6 a.m. to AVOID the rush hour.

(2) You can *avoid doing something* yourself but you *prevent someone else (from) doing something*.

Hablaban en voz baja para no despertar al niño.	⊗They spoke quietly to prevent waking the baby.⊗ They spoke quietly to AVOID waking the baby.
Han puesto una barandilla para que no se caiga la gente.	⊗They have put up a handrail to avoid people falling.⊗ They have put up a handrail to PREVENT people falling.

B

Bad(ly)

Bad is an adjective only: the adverb form is *badly*.

Canta muy mal.	⊗He sings very bad.⊗ He sings very BADLY.

Hablo muy mal el inglés.	⊗I speak very bad the English.⊗ I speak very BAD English. (I speak English very BADLY.)
El trabajo está muy mal pagado.	⊗The job is very bad paid.⊗ The job is very BADLY paid.

Bath

To have a bath means at home, in the bathroom. *To bathe* means in the sea/river etc., though *to swim/to go for a swim/to have a swim* are more common.

Me bañé porque el agua estaba caliente.	⊗The sea was very warm, so I had a bath.⊗ The sea was very warm, so I HAD A SWIM. (I WENT FOR A SWIM.)
Tomo un baño cada día antes de ir al trabajo.	⊗I bathe every morning before going to work.⊗ I HAVE A BATH every morning before going to work.

To be used to

See USED TO

Because (of)

Because is used before a clause (i.e. with a verb and subject); *because of* is a preposition, used before a noun or pronoun.

Dejaron de jugar a causa de la lluvia.	⊗They stopped playing because of it was raining.⊗ They stopped playing BECAUSE it was raining. (BECAUSE OF THE RAIN.)
Llegó tarde porque los autobuses estaban en huelga.	⊗She arrived late because the bus strike.⊗ She arrived late because OF the bus strike.

Been

Been and *gone* are both used as past participles of *to go*, but *been* normally means that somebody went and came back; *gone* means that the person is not here now.

¿Has estado alguna vez en Londres?	⊗Have you ever gone to London?⊗ Have you ever BEEN to London?
No está en casa. ¿Adónde ha ido?	⊗He's not at home – where has he been?⊗ He's not at home – where has he GONE?
Vengo de comprar.	⊗I've just gone shopping.⊗ I've just BEEN shopping.

N.B. *Been* is also used when a person is still in a place and you are talking to him/her in that place:

¿Has estado antes en Londres?	Have you BEEN to London before? (We are speaking in London now.)

Before

See also AFTER, (IN) FRONT (OF)

(1) The main errors with *before* correspond almost exactly to those with *after*, with a slight difference in case no. 1, where we use *before that/this*.

Salieron de casa; antes, habían visto el partido en la televisión.	⊗They went out; before, they had watched the match on TV.⊗
	They went out; BEFORE THAT, they had watched the match on TV.

(2) In addition, *before* is rarely used as a preposition of place; instead, we use *in front of* or *outside* according to the example.

Estaba delante de la puerta.	⊗He was standing before the door.⊗
	He was standing IN FRONT OF the door.

Best

Best is the superlative of *good*. The preposition normally used with it is *in*. *Better* is the comparative form, used with *than*.

El café es la mejor bebida del mundo.	⊗Coffee is the better drink of the world.⊗
	Coffee is the BEST drink IN the world.
Para mí, McEnroe es mejor que Connors.	⊗I think McEnroe is better that Connors.⊗
	I think McEnroe is BETTER THAN Connors.

Better, you had

The expression *you had (you'd) better* is used, without *to*, when giving somebody advice.

Sería mejor que te acostaras si te encuentras mal.	⊗You/You'd better to go to bed if you're feeling ill.⊗
	YOU'D BETTER GO to bed if you're feeling ill.

Between

Between is used when there are 2 (or more) objects which we can see and distinguish clearly from each other; *among* is for groups of people and things which we cannot clearly separate.

Estaba sentado entre John y Peter.	⊗He was sitting among John and Peter.⊗
	He was sitting BETWEEN John and Peter.
Vivío 2 años entre los indios del Amazonas.	⊗She lived for 2 years between the Amazon Indians.⊗
	She lived for 2 years AMONG the Amazon Indians.

Luxemburgo se encuentra entre Francia, Alemania y Bélgica.

⊗Luxemburg is among France, Germany and Belgium.⊗

Luxemburg is BETWEEN France, Germany and Belgium.

Bored, boring

See ADJECTIVES (4)

To be born

Born is used with different tenses of the verb *to be*, from which it is inseparable. It cannot be used like an ordinary verb - for example, it does not change its form in other tenses, nor is it used with the auxiliary verbs *do* or *did*.

¿Dónde naciste?

⊗Where did you born?⊗

Where WERE YOU BORN?

Nació en 1960.

⊗He borned in 1960.⊗

He WAS BORN in 1960.

En el futuro, habrá más niños que nacerán en casa.

⊗In the future, more children will born at home.⊗

In the future, more children WILL BE BORN at home.

To borrow

This verb is often confused with *to lend*. *To borrow* is to take for a time from somebody; *to lend* is to give for a time to somebody.

¿Puedes prestarme £5?

⊗Can you borrow me £5?⊗

Can you LEND me £5?

¿Me dejas tu libro?

⊗Can I lend your book?⊗

Can I BORROW your book?

(Can you LEND ME your book?)

Sus padres les dejaron dinero.

⊗They borrowed money to their parents.⊗

They borrowed money FROM their parents.

(or: Their parents LENT THEM money.)

Both

(1) For the normal position of *both* in a sentence, see WORD ORDER (2).

Ambos son franceses.

⊗They both are French.⊗

They ARE BOTH French.

Nos gusta nadar (a ambos).

⊗We like both swimming.⊗

We BOTH LIKE swimming.

Ambos han estado en Turquía.

⊗They both have been to Turkey.⊗

They HAVE BOTH BEEN to Turkey.

(2) *Both* cannot have an article in front of it.

Los dos hombres fueron detenidos.

⊗The both men were arrested.⊗

BOTH men were arrested.

(3) It cannot be used without *of* before a personal pronoun.

Vamos a correr los dos cada día.	⊗Both we go running every day.⊗ BOTH OF US go running every day.

(4) When used before a noun, it can be followed by *of* only when there is an article (e.g. the), a possessive (e.g. my), or a demonstrative (e.g. these).

Los dos coches se averiaron.	⊗Both of cars broke down.⊗ BOTH (OF) THE CARS broke down.

To break

(1) *To break* is for solid things, e.g. the TV, a chair, your leg. When we talk about non-solid things, e.g. paper, material, clothes, we use *to tear*.

Rompió la hoja en 4 trozos.	⊗He broke the paper into 4 pieces.⊗ He TORE the paper into 4 pieces.
Al sentarse, la silla se le rompió.	The chair BROKE when he sat on it.

(2) When talking about a car with mechanical problems, we don't use *to break* but *to break down*, or *not to work*, *not to go*, etc.

Se le averió el coche en la autopista.	⊗His car broke/was broken on the motorway.⊗ His car BROKE DOWN on the motorway.
Mi coche no funciona.	⊗My car is broken at the moment.⊗ My car ISN'T WORKING/ISN'T GOING at the moment.

To bring

To bring is often confused with *to take*. *To bring* means movement towards the person who is speaking. *To take* means movement away from the person who is speaking.

(A friend rings John's house. John's wife answers the phone.)

–John no está, ha llevado a los niños al zoo.	⊗"John's not here – he has brought the children to the zoo."⊗ "John's not here – he has TAKEN the children to the zoo."
¿Puedes traerme tabaco cuando vengas?	⊗Can you take me some cigarettes when you come?⊗ Can you BRING me some cigarettes when you come?

Brothers

Brothers, the plural of *brother*, is masculine only. When referring to both sexes, we use *brothers and sisters*.

Tengo 2 hermanos, Paul y Silvia.	⊗I have 2 brothers, Paul and Sylvia.⊗ I have ONE BROTHER, Paul, and ONE SISTER, Sylvia.
¿Tienes hermanos?	Have you got any BROTHERS or SISTERS?

To buy

To buy must have an object; if the object is not specified, we normally use the expression *to go shopping* or *to do some shopping*.

Fue a comprar al mercado.	⊗She went to buy at the market.⊗ She WENT SHOPPING at the market.
Tengo que ir a comprar.	⊗I must go out to buy.⊗ I must GO (OUT) SHOPPING. (I must DO SOME SHOPPING.)

C

To call

In normal English, we don't use *to call* when speaking about someone's name. It is used more often for people's *nicknames* ('motes').

¿Cómo se llama?	⊗How is he called?⊗ WHAT IS HIS NAME?
Lo llaman "el león" porque tiene mucho coraje.	He is CALLED "The Lion" because he is very brave.

Camping

In English, *camping* is the activity, not a place where people camp – this is a *campsite*.

Dormimos en un camping muy bonito.	⊗We stayed at a nice camping.⊗ We stayed on/at a nice CAMPSITE.
Hacemos camping todos los veranos.	We GO CAMPING every summer.

Can

(1) Like almost all modal auxiliary verbs, *can* is never used with *to*, *do* or *did*, and has no infinitive or participles. See MODAL AUXILIARY VERBS.

¿Sabes nadar?	⊗Can you to swim?⊗ Can you SWIM?

(2) *Can* is not used with *will* for a future action. For a future action, we must use *will be able to*.

Cumpliré 18 años en marzo, y entonces podré sacarme el permiso de conducir.	⊗I'll be 18 in March; I'll can get a driving licence then.⊗ I'll be 18 in March; I'll BE ABLE TO get a driving licence then.

(3) *Can* is only used for a general possibility – something which is some-

times possible or generally true. For a possibility referring to a specific occasion, we must use *may*, *might*, or *could*.

Está nublado – puede que llueva esta tarde.	⊗It's very cloudy – it can rain this afternoon.⊗ It's very cloudy – it MAY/MIGHT/COULD rain this afternoon. (specific time)
Normalmente agosto es el mes más seco, pero puede ocurrir que llueva mucho.	August is normally the driest month, but it CAN rain heavily. (sometimes true)

To care

The expression *I don't care* is often confused with *I don't mind*. *I don't care* means that something is not of importance or interest to the speaker. *I don't mind* means *I don't object to/dislike*.

Puede decir lo que quiera; sencillamente, no me importa.	⊗He can say what he likes – I just don't mind.⊗ He can say what he likes – I just don't CARE.
¿Te molesta/importa que fume?	⊗Do you care if I smoke?⊗ Do you MIND if I smoke?

Career

In English, your *career* begins after you leave school or University and start work as a professional person. At University, you *do* or *study* a course or subject.

¿Qué carrera estudia?	⊗What career is he studying?⊗ What SUBJECT is he STUDYING? (What COURSE is he DOING?)
Tuvo una excelente vida profesional: durante 30 años fue una destacada abogada.	She had a wonderful CAREER: she was a top lawyer for 30 years.

To carry

To carry normally means in your hands or arms, usually with the idea of movement. *To hold* is similar but without the idea of movement. *To take* translates 'llevar' with the idea of transport (particularly a car). *To wear* is for clothes.

Te llevaré a la estación.	⊗I'll carry you to the station.⊗ I'll TAKE you to the station.
¿Qué llevas/tienes en la mano?	⊗What are you wearing (in your hands)?⊗ What are you CARRYING/HOLDING?
Los carteros tienen que llevar sacos llenos de cartas.	⊗Postmen have to hold sacks full of letters.⊗ Postmen have to CARRY sacks full of letters.

Lleva (puesto) un nuevo vestido.	⊗She is carrying a new dress.⊗ She is WEARING a new dress.

Case, in

In case is a precaution and normally translates 'por si (acaso)'. But it does not translate 'en el caso de que . . .', which is a conditional:

Si perdemos el tren, tendremos que ir en autocar.	⊗In case we miss the train, we'll have to go by coach.⊗ IF we miss the train, we'll have to go by coach.
Llévate el paraguas por si llueve.	Take your umbrella IN CASE it rains.

To catch

To catch has 2 common meanings.
(1) *To catch* the bus, train, plane etc.

Cogió el tren de las 17.30.	He CAUGHT the 5.30 train.

(2) *To catch* something that is thrown, e.g. a ball. It does not translate 'coger' with objects like book, umbrella, pen etc. (unless these objects are thrown!). We say *to pick up* for an object which is lying on a table/floor/shelf etc. If we pick up an object with the intention of going out with it, we normally use *to take*.

Cogió el bolígrafo y empezó a escribir una carta.	⊗He caught his pen and started writing a letter.⊗ He PICKED UP his pen and started writing a letter.
Cogió su talonario para ir de compras.	⊗He caught his cheque-book to go shopping.⊗ He TOOK his cheque-book to go shopping.
El portero atrapó la pelota.	The goalkeeper CAUGHT the ball.

To celebrate

We *celebrate* a special occasion, e.g. Christmas, someone's birthday, a wedding anniversary etc. Events such as a party, a concert or a meeting cannot be *celebrated*; instead, we normally use an expression like *to have/hold*, *to take place* or *to be held* (passive).

El concierto se celebró en el parque.	⊗The concert was celebrated in the park.⊗ The concert WAS HELD/TOOK PLACE in the park.
En Navidad celebramos una fiesta.	⊗We celebrated a party for Christmas.⊗ We HAD/HELD a party for Christmas. (We HAD a party TO CELEBRATE Christmas).
Los aficionados celebraron haber ganado la copa.	The supporters CELEBRATED (their team) winning the Cup.

Chance

Chance means *opportunity*, not *luck*.

¡Qué suerte! ¡Has ganado un coche nuevo!	⊗What (a) chance! You've won a new car!⊗
	What LUCK! You've won a new car!
¡Qué oportunidad! ¡No te ofrecen cada día la posibilidad de trabajar en Los Angeles!	What a CHANCE! – it's not every day you get the opportunity to work in L.A.!

To change

To change is not followed by *of*. We usually talk of *changing your mind*, not of *changing an idea*.

Al principio me gustaba la idea pero ahora he cambiado de opinión.	⊗At first I liked the idea, but now I've changed of idea/opinion.⊗
	At first I liked the idea, but now I've changed MY MIND.

Christmas

The different prepositions used with *Christmas* always cause problems. We say *at Christmas* but *on Christmas Day/Eve* (a specific day) and *in/during the Christmas holidays*.

En Navidad se reune toda la familia.	⊗In Christmas, all the family gets together.⊗
	AT Christmas, all the family gets together.
El día de Navidad hacemos una comida especial.	⊗We have a special meal in/the Christmas Day.⊗
	We have a special meal ON Christmas Day.
¿Qué hiciste durante las vacaciones de Navidad?	What did you do IN/DURING the Christmas holidays?

Cold See also HOT

(1) In English, we always use the verb *to be*, not *to have*, with adjectives of temperature (cold, hot, warm, cool), for people, objects and the weather. *To have a cold* means 'estar resfriado'.

Pasé frío durante la noche.	⊗I had cold during the night.⊗
	I WAS/FELT cold during the night.
Hace frío esta tarde.	⊗It have/has cold this afternoon.⊗
	It IS cold this afternoon.
No voy a bañarme: el agua está demasiado fría.	I'm not going for a swim: the water IS too cold.
Es una persona muy fría.	He IS a very cold person.

(2) *Cold* is an extreme of temperature and usually has a negative connotation. *Cool* means *not warm* or *less warm* and can have both a positive and a negative sense.

Después de un día muy caluroso, por la noche suele hacer fresco.	⊗After a really hot day, the evening is often cold.⊗ After a really hot day, the evening is often COOL. (i.e. a positive thing)
Hace fresco esta mañana, ¿no?	It's a bit COOL this morning, isn't it? (i.e. a negative thing)
Esta sopa está muy caliente: voy a dejar que se enfríe un poco.	⊗This soup is too hot: I'm going to let it get cold.⊗ This soup is too hot: I'm going to let it COOL (down).
En invierno, las noches son muy frías.	In winter, the nights are really COLD.

To come

(1) Generally, *to come* is used for movement towards the place where the speaker or listener is; *to go* is generally used for movement to another place.

Es tarde, tengo que volver a casa.	⊗It's late – I must come home.⊗ It's late – I must GO home.
–John, ya está la cena. *–Vale, voy.*	"John, your dinner's ready." ⊗"O.K., I'm going."⊗ "O.K., I'm COMING."
Vengo al trabajo en autobús.	I COME to work by bus. (you are in the office now)
Voy al trabajo en autobús.	I GO to work by bus. (you are in another place)

(2) But notice we say *to come with* when we mean *to accompany* the speaker to a place.

Voy a una fiesta el próximo sábado. ¿Quieres venir (conmigo)?	⊗I'm going to a party on Saturday – would you like to go with me?⊗ I'm going to a party on Saturday – would you like to COME with me?

To come from

To talk about the city or country where someone was born or educated, we can use *to come from* or *to be from*. In the interrogative form, *to come from* takes the normal auxiliary verb *do/did*, but *to be from* does not.

¿De dónde eres?	⊗Where are you come from?⊗ ⊗Where do you are from?⊗ Where DO YOU COME from? Where ARE YOU from?
Soy italiano.	⊗I am come from Italy.⊗ I AM from Italy. (I COME FROM Italy.)

Comprehensive

Comprehensive in English means *including everything*; to describe a person who can understand other people's problems, we use *understanding*.

Mi jefe se mostró muy comprensivo cuando le expliqué el problema.	⊗My boss was very comprehensive when I told him the problem.⊗
	My boss was very UNDERSTANDING when I told him the problem.
Han hecho un nuevo estudio exhaustivo sobre el gorila.	A new, COMPREHENSIVE study of the gorilla has been made/produced.

To concentrate

The verb *to concentrate* is not used reflexively.

Tuve que concentrarme para seguir la conferencia.	⊗I had to concentrate myself to follow the lecture.⊗
	I had to CONCENTRATE to follow the lecture.

Conductor

In English, a *conductor* is either (a) the leader of an orchestra or (b) the man who collects fares and distributes tickets on a bus. To translate 'conductor', we say *driver*.

Hay demasiados conductores que no respetan las señales de tráfico.	⊗Too many conductors ignore traffic signs.⊗
	Too many MOTORISTS/DRIVERS ignore traffic signs.
Von Karajan es un director sensacional.	Von Karajan is a wonderful CONDUCTOR.
En este autobús no cobra el conductor: pasará el cobrador.	You don't pay the driver on this bus: the CONDUCTOR will come round (for the fares).

Contaminated

We use *polluted/pollution* when talking about dirt in the air/sea etc. (i.e. they have been made dirty). *Contaminated* has a much more specific meaning, when something (usually food or drink) has been infected by an organism.

Todas las playas estaban contaminadas.	⊗The beaches were all contaminated.⊗
	The beaches were all POLLUTED.
No comas esa carne – está contaminada.	Don't eat that meat – it's CONTAMINATED.

Continual

Continual is used for an action which is repeated frequently; *Continuous* is used for an action which does not stop.

No aguanto todas estas continuas discusiones.	⊗I can't stand all these continuous arguments.⊗
	I can't stand all these CONTINUAL arguments.
Había un movimiento continuo de tráfico.	⊗There was a continual flow of traffic.⊗
	There was a CONTINUOUS flow of traffic.

Contractions

Contractions between a subject and auxiliary verb (or *to be*) or between an auxiliary verb and *not*, are common, e.g. I can't, I've got, she's not, they haven't seen etc. However there are exceptions.

(1) These cannot be used in the affirmative form when there is no principal verb following.

–¿Has estado en París?	"Have you been to Paris?"
–Sí, (he estado).	⊗"Yes, I've."⊗
	"Yes, I HAVE." ("Yes, I'VE BEEN there.")
–¿Vienes a la fiesta el sábado que viene?	"Are you coming to the party next Saturday?"
–Sí, vengo.	⊗"Yes, I'm."⊗
	"Yes, I AM." ("Yes, I'M COMING.")

(2) The verb *to have* is only contracted when it is an auxiliary, not a principal, verb, unless used with *got*.

Tengo un coche nuevo.	⊗I've a new car.⊗
	I'VE GOT a new car. (I HAVE a new car.)

Cook, cooker, cooking

(1) *A cook* is the person who cooks.

Mi madre cocina muy bien.	⊗My mother is a wonderful cooker.⊗
	My mother is a wonderful COOK.

(2) *A cooker* is the machine: *kitchen* is the room where *a cooker* is used.

Acabamos de comprar una nueva cocina.	⊗We've just bought a new cook/kitchen.⊗
	We've just bought a new COOKER.
La cocina es más grande que el salón.	The KITCHEN is bigger than the living-room.

(3) *Cooking* is the hobby or interest.

Mis hobbies son cocinar y leer.	⊗My hobbies are cook and read.⊗
	My hobbies are COOKING and READING.

(4) *A cookery book* is full of recipes and instructions.

¿Has visto este nuevo libro de cocina?	⊗Have you seen this new cooking book?⊗
	Have you seen this new COOKERY book?

To cost

The most common mistake with this verb is to use it in the interrogative form without the auxiliary verb *do/does/did* or with the verb *to be*.

¿Cuánto cuesta este jersey?	⊗How much costs this jumper?⊗
	⊗How much this jumper costs?⊗
	How much DOES this jumper COST? (How much IS this jumper?)
¿Cuánto te costó la entrada?	⊗How much was cost/costed/did cost the ticket?⊗
	How much DID the ticket COST? (How much WAS the ticket?)

Could See also MODAL AUXILIARY VERBS

The most common mistake with *could* is when it is used in the past for ability to do something. In this context, it is only used for general ability, for something which you could always do, and not for ability on a specific occasion – for this, we must use *was/were able to*, *managed to . . .* or *succeeded in (doing)*.

Era una noche oscura, y 3 reclusos pudieron/lograron escapar.	⊗It was a dark night, and 3 prisoners could escape.⊗
	It was a dark night, and 3 prisoners WERE ABLE TO/MANAGED TO escape.
El examen era muy difícil, pero pude/logré aprobar.	⊗The exam was very hard, but I could pass.⊗
	The exam was very hard, but I WAS ABLE TO/MANAGED TO pass.
A los 5 años ya sabía nadar.	I COULD swim even when I was five.

To cry

To cry normally means 'llorar' (although it sometimes means 'gritar', e.g. in literary English or in direct speech). The normal translation of 'gritar' is *to shout*.

¡No grites! Te oigo perfectamente.	⊗Don't cry! I can hear you perfectly well!⊗
	Don't SHOUT! I can hear you perfectly well!
¡Es terrible! ¡Mis vecinos siempre gritan!	⊗It's terrible! My neighbours are always crying!⊗
	It's terrible! My neighbours are always SHOUTING!
-¡No me dejes sola!-gritó.	"Don't leave me on my own!" she CRIED.
¿Qué te pasa? ¿Por qué lloras?	What's the matter? Why are you CRYING?

Curious

In English, we generally use *curious* to talk about a person who has curiosity to find out about places, or other people; to translate the idea of 'curioso/extraño' we use *strange* or *unusual*.

Es un tipo curioso: nunca le comprenderé.	⊗He's a curious person: I'll never understand him.⊗
	He's a STRANGE person: I'll never understand him.
Tiene mucha curiosidad: siempre quiere saber todo lo que pasa.	He's very CURIOUS: he always wants to know what's going on.

D

To damage

To damage is normally used for things; *to hurt* or *to injure* for people; *to wound* means with a gun or knife, and it is never an accident.

Se cayó y se hizo daño en el brazo.	⊗He fell over and damaged his arm.⊗
	He fell over and INJURED/HURT his arm.
3 personas resultaron heridas en el accidente.	⊗3 people were damaged in the accident.⊗
	3 people were INJURED/HURT in the accident.
El soldado fue herido por una bala.	⊗The soldier was hurt/damaged by a bullet.⊗
	The soldier was WOUNDED by a bullet.
Centenares de edificios sufrieron daños en el terremoto.	Hundreds of buildings were DAMAGED in the earthquake.

Dead

Dead is an adjective; *to die* (past form: *died*) is a verb; *death* is a noun.

Murió en un accidente de coche.	⊗He was died/dead in a car crash.⊗
	He DIED (or He WAS KILLED) in a car crash.
Los médicos intentaron salvarle, pero ya estaba/había muerto.	⊗The doctors tried to save him but he was already died.⊗
	The doctors tried to save him but he was already DEAD.
¿Tienes miedo a morir/a la muerte?	⊗Are you afraid of die?⊗
	Are you afraid of DEATH/DYING?

To deceive

This verb translates 'engañar'. It is often confused with *to disappoint*, which means 'decepcionar'.

Me decepcionó mucho la película. ⊗I was very deceived with the film.⊗
I was very DISAPPOINTED with the film.

Me engañó: me robó todo el dinero. ⊗He disappointed me: he stole all my money.⊗
He DECEIVED me: he stole all my money.

To deny

To deny and *to refuse* are often confused. Basically, *to deny* corresponds to 'negar', and *to refuse* to 'negarse (a hacer)' or 'rechazar'. *To deny* always refers to a present or past situation and is not followed by an infinitive but by the present (or present perfect) participle, or by a full subject and verb in the Past or Past Perfect. *To refuse* is followed by a noun or the infinitive of a verb, and refers to a future action or situation.

Se negó a ayudarme. ⊗She denied to help me.⊗
She REFUSED to help me.

Rechazó la oferta de la empresa. ⊗He denied the company's offer.⊗
He REFUSED the company's offer.

Negó haber robado las joyas. ⊗He refused stealing the jewels.⊗
He DENIED stealing/having stolen/that he had stolen the jewels.

Negaron ser espías. ⊗They refused that they were spies.⊗
They DENIED being/that they were spies.

To depend

The preposition used with this verb is *on* and not *of*.

–¿Adónde vas de vacaciones? "Where are you going for your holidays?"
–No sé, depende del dinero. ⊗"I don't know, it depends of the money."⊗
"I don't know, it depends ON the money."

Despite

This means the same as *in spite of* but notice that *of* is not used with *despite*.

A pesar del mal tiempo, disfrutamos de las vacaciones. ⊗Despite of the bad weather, we enjoyed the holiday.⊗
DESPITE the bad weather, we enjoyed the holiday.

Director

The usual meaning of *director* in English is a member of the board of a company. In most cases where Spanish uses *director*, a different word is used in English.

Es el director de un conocido(a) colegio/periódico/orquesta.	⊗He's the director of a famous school/newspaper/orchestra.⊗
	He's the HEADMASTER/EDITOR/CONDUCTOR of a famous school/newspaper/orchestra.
Ascendió puestos en la empresa hasta llegar a ser uno de los directivos.	He worked his way up the company until he became one of the DIRECTORS.

To discuss

This verb means *to talk about* or *to comment on* something. When 2 or more people don't agree, we use *to argue* or *to have an argument*.

¡Es terrible! ¡Mis vecinos siempre están discutiendo!	⊗It's terrible! My neighbours are always discussing!⊗
	It's terrible! My neighbours are always ARGUING!
Ayer tuve una fuerte discusión con mi padre.	⊗I had a big discussion with my father yesterday.⊗
	I had a big ARGUMENT with my father yesterday.
Hablamos de la situación y llegamos a la misma conclusión.	We DISCUSSED the situation and reached the same conclusion.
Al salir del teatro tuvimos una charla muy interesante sobre la obra.	After leaving the theatre, we had a very interesting DISCUSSION about the play.

Disgusted

(1) This adjective has a much stronger meaning than the Spanish 'disgustado'; it means 'asqueado' or 'horrorizado'.

Estaba disgustado porque empezó a llover.	⊗He was disgusted because it started raining.⊗
	He was ANNOYED because it started raining.
Le horrorizó la violencia empleada por la policía.	He was DISGUSTED by the violence shown by the police.

(2) See ADJECTIVES (4).

To do   See also TO MAKE

It is very difficult to distinguish between *to do* and *to make*.

(1) *Do* is normally used when work is mentioned.

Tengo mucho trabajo (que hacer).	⊗I have a lot of work to make.⊗
	I have a lot of work to DO.
¿Has hecho los deberes?	⊗Have you made the homework?⊗
	Have you DONE the homework?

Odio el trabajo de la casa. ⊗I hate making housework.⊗
I hate DOING housework.

(2) *Do* is normally used when no specific activity is mentioned.

¡Haz algo! ⊗Make something!⊗
DO something!

¿Qué hiciste durante las vacaciones? ⊗What did you make in the holidays?⊗
What did you DO in the holidays?

(3) *Make* is normally used when the meaning is *create* or *construct*.

Acabo de hacer un pastel. ⊗I have just done a cake.⊗
I have just MADE a cake.

Estoy haciendo un marco para la foto. ⊗I'm doing a frame for the photo.⊗
I'm MAKING a frame for the photo.

(4) In other cases, there are no clear rules.

tratar/negociar con — TO DO business with
hacer algo lo mejor posible — TO DO one's best
hacer un favor a alguién — TO DO someone a favour
hacer el bien — TO DO good

To do (question)

The question *What do you do*? refers to a person's profession. To ask about someone's activities at the moment/now, we say *What are you doing*?

–¿Qué estás haciendo?
–Estoy escuchando la radio.

⊗"What do you do?"⊗
"I'm listening to the radio."
"What ARE YOU DOING?"
"I'm listening to the radio."

–¿A qué te dedicas?
–Soy arquitecto.

"What DO YOU DO?"
"I'm an architect."

To dream

(1) The preposition used with this verb is *about* or *of* and not *with*. Note that two past forms exist, *dreamed* and *dreamt*.

Anoche soñé contigo. ⊗I dreamed with you last night.⊗
I dreamed ABOUT/OF you last night.

(2) When *dream* means *imagine*, the usual preposition is *of*.

Jamás imaginé estar en una isla tan bella. ⊗I never dreamt with being on such a beautiful island.⊗
I never dreamt OF being on such a beautiful island.

To dress

To dress is often confused with *to wear* and *to put on*. You cannot *dress clothes*; we say *to be dressed in . . .* or *to wear* clothes. You can *dress* another person (usually a child or a very old person) but we do not normally say *to dress yourself* – for this, we use simply *to dress* or, more commonly, *to get dressed*. *To put on clothes* is the act of getting dressed.

Llevaba una blusa roja.	⊗She dressed a red blouse.⊗
	She WAS DRESSED IN/WAS WEARING a red blouse.
Viste muy elegantemente.	⊗He wears very smartly.⊗
	He DRESSES very smartly.
Voy a vestir al niño.	I'm going to DRESS the baby.
¿Cuánto tardas en vestirte?	How long do you take to GET DRESSED?
Siempre se pone el pantalón antes que la camisa.	⊗He always wears his trousers before his shirt.⊗
	He always PUTS ON his trousers before his shirt.

During

During does not indicate the duration of an action (we say *for* 3 weeks/6 days/8 months etc.) but refers to a period of time when or within which an action takes place.

Estudió durante 3 horas.	⊗He studied during 3 hours.⊗
	He studied FOR 3 hours.
Mi hermano estuvo ingresado 2 semanas.	⊗My brother was in hospital during 2 weeks.⊗
	My brother was in hospital FOR 2 weeks.
Durante el verano, a veces vamos a navegar.	DURING the summer, we SOMETIMES go sailing.
Compró su nuevo coche durante las vacaciones de Navidad.	He bought his new car DURING the Christmas holidays.

E

Each

In many cases *each* has a very similar meaning to *every* – see EVERY. However, *each* cannot be used after words like *almost*, *nearly*, *practically* or in expressions like *every 3 days*, *every 6 months* etc..

La veo casi todos los días.	⊗I see her almost each day.⊗
	I see her almost EVERY day.
Casi todas las casas de esta manzana tienen calefacción central.	⊗Nearly each house in this block has central heating.⊗
	Nearly EVERY house in this block has central heating.

El Mundial de fútbol se celebra cada 4 años.	⊗The World Cup is held each 4 years.⊗ The World Cup is held EVERY four years.

Early

Early means *at an early hour* or *before the time expected. Soon* means *within a short time* and is always used in a future sense at the time of speaking.

Pronto llegaremos: sólo faltan unos 15 kilómetros.	⊗Only another 10 miles: we'll be there early.⊗ Only another 10 miles: we'll be there SOON.
El tren llegó con 10 minutos de antelación.	⊗The train arrived 10 minutes soon.⊗ The train arrived 10 minutes EARLY.
Me gusta levantarme temprano.	⊗I like to get up soon.⊗ I like to get up EARLY.

Economic(al)

Economic refers to the economy/money situation etc. *Economical* means *cheap to maintain or use.*

La situación económica está muy mal.	⊗The economical situation is very bad.⊗ The ECONOMIC situation is very bad.
Nuestro nuevo coche resulta muy económico. *(Gasta muy poco)*	Our new car is very ECONOMICAL.

Embarrassed

(1) It is confused with *embarrassing* in the same way as *bored/boring* – see ADJECTIVES (4).

Era una situación embarazosa.	⊗It was a very embarrassed situation.⊗ It was a very EMBARRASSING situation.

(2) A woman expecting a baby is not *embarrassed* but *pregnant*. You feel *embarrassed* e.g. when you say something stupid in public.

Mi hermana está embarazada por segunda vez.	⊗My sister is embarrassed for the second time.⊗ My sister is PREGNANT for the second time.
Fue muy violento, no pude acordarme de su nombre.	I felt so EMBARRASSED when I couldn't remember his name.

End

In the end means *finally*, when something happens after a certain time. *At the end* is always followed by *of* and can be used in the sense of both time (e.g. *at the end* of the film) and distance (e.g. *at the end* of the street).

Al final de la clase fuimos a tomar algo.	⊗In the end of the class, we went for a drink.⊗
	AT the end of the class, we went for a drink.
Se presentó al examen 4 veces y finalmente logró aprobar.	⊗He took the exam 4 times and, at the end, managed to pass.⊗
	He took the exam 4 times and IN the end, managed to pass.

To enjoy

(1) A verb following *to enjoy* must be in the '-ing' form, not in the infinitive.

Le gusta leer.	⊗He enjoys read/to read.⊗
	He enjoys READING.

(2) It must have an object.

-¿Pasaste unas buenas vacaciones?	"Did you have a nice holiday?"
-Sí, me divertí mucho.	⊗"Yes, I enjoyed a lot."⊗
	"Yes, I enjoyed IT a lot."

(3) The past form *enjoyed* cannot be used as an adjective; the adjectival form is *enjoyable*.

Era una película muy divertida.	⊗It was a very enjoyed film.⊗
	It was a very ENJOYABLE film.

(4) A person can enjoy a thing but not vice-versa. (see also TO LIKE (4))

Me gustó mucho la obra.	⊗The play enjoyed me very much.⊗
	I ENJOYED THE PLAY very much.

Enough

Enough usually comes before a noun but after an adjective or adverb.

No tiene la edad para ir al colegio.	⊗She isn't enough old to go to school.⊗
	She isn't OLD ENOUGH to go to school.
No tenemos suficiente dinero para comprar un coche nuevo.	⊗We haven't (got) money enough to buy a new car.⊗
	We haven't (got) ENOUGH MONEY to buy a new car.

Especially   See SPECIALLY

Eventual

The adjective *eventual* is very similar in meaning to *final*; similarly, the adverb *eventually* has the meaning of *finally* or *in the end*. To translate the Spanish 'eventual' we say *temporary* or *for the moment*.

Tiene un trabajo eventual.	⊗He has an eventual job.⊗
	He has a TEMPORARY job.
Tardó 10 horas pero, por fin, llegó a Londres.	It took him 10 hours, but EVENTUALLY he got to London.

Ever

Ever means *at any time*. It is often confused with *never*, which means *at no time* (see NEVER) and with *always*, which means *at all times* or *all the time*. (But notice *for ever* and *ever since*).

Siempre me acuesto temprano.	⊗I ever go to bed early.⊗ I ALWAYS go to bed early.
Si alguna vez necesitas ayuda sólo tienes que llamarme.	If you EVER need any help, just ring me.
Siempre te amaré.	I will love you FOREVER/FOR EVER. (I will ALWAYS love you.)
Está deprimido desde que su madre murió.	He has been depressed EVER SINCE his mother died.

Every

(1) For the difference between *every* and *all*, see ALL.
(2) *Every* is very similar to *each*, but *every* puts people or things into a group and *each* separates them.

Todos los jugadores hicieron una gran labor.	EVERY player worked hard. (ALL THE players worked hard.)
Uno a uno, todos los jugadores fueron presentados a la reina.	⊗Every player was introduced to the Queen in turn.⊗ EACH player was introduced to the Queen in turn.

(3) *Every* never refers to only 2 people or things.

Cada gemelo tiene su propia personalidad.	⊗Every of the twins has his own personality.⊗ EACH of the twins has his own personality.

To excuse

Excuse me is normally used before, not after, we do something which might annoy other people, e.g. if we ask people to stand up to let us pass in the cinema or on the bus, or before we interrupt someone's conversation. We normally use *sorry* to apologise after we do something which might have annoyed another person; and also to ask someone to repeat something we didn't hear or understand the first time.

–Ésta es una zona de no fumadores.	"This is a non-smoking area."
–Ay, perdón, no lo sabía.	⊗"Oh, excuse me, I didn't know."⊗ "Oh SORRY, I didn't know."
–Perdone, no le entiendo.	⊗"Excuse me, I don't understand you."⊗ "SORRY, I don't understand you."
¿Me dejaría pasar, por favor?	"EXCUSE ME, could I get past, please?"

To expect

This verb is often confused with *to hope* and *to wait*. There are three basic differences.
(1) *To expect* is used for an idea which is very logical or when we are sure something will happen.

Está esperando un niño.	⊗She is waiting (for) a baby.⊗ She is EXPECTING a baby.
Seguro que hará calor en Kenia.	⊗I hope it will be hot in Kenya.⊗ I EXPECT it will be hot in Kenya.
Un día de éstos tiene que llegar una felicitación de mis padres.	⊗I am hoping a birthday card from my parents soon.⊗ I am EXPECTING a birthday card from my parents soon.

(2) *To hope* is simply to express a wish.

Espero recibir una respuesta pronto.	I am HOPING FOR a reply soon. (But I am not sure about it.)
Espero que no haga (demasiado) frío este invierno.	⊗I expect it won't be cold this winter.⊗ I HOPE it won't be cold this winter. (But it probably will be cold.)
Espero que te mejores pronto.	⊗I expect you get better soon.⊗ I HOPE you get better soon.

(3) *To wait (for)* is used with the idea of time passing, often when we talk about somebody being too late or too early.

¡Te esperé durante 25 minutos!	⊗I expected/was expecting you for 25 minutes!⊗ I WAITED FOR you for 25 minutes!

To explain

(1) This verb cannot be followed immediately by an indirect noun or pronoun object.

¿Puedes explicarme el problema?	⊗Can you explain me the problem?⊗ Can you EXPLAIN the problem (to me)?

(2) *Explicate* does not exist!!

Ya te lo explicaré todo (sobre el problema) cuando vuelva.	⊗I will explicate you everything (about the problem) when I get back.⊗ I will EXPLAIN everything (about the problem) when I get back.

(3) You can *explain* a problem or a situation or why you did something, but not a story, an exam, your holiday etc..

¡Explícame lo que hiciste en Grecia durante las vacaciones!	⊗Explain me all about your holiday in Greece!⊗ TELL me all about your holiday in Greece!
Dínos/Explícanos como te fue el examen.	⊗Explain us how you got on in the exam.⊗ TELL us how you got on in the exam.

F

Familiar

Familiar in English does not refer to the family; it means a person or thing that you know very well/have seen many times etc..

El día de Navidad siempre celebramos una fiesta familiar.	⊗On Christmas Day, we always have a familiar party.⊗ On Christmas Day, we always have a FAMILY party.
Ya conozco muy bien Roma porque he estado muchas veces.	I've been to Rome so many times it's FAMILIAR to me now.

Far

(1) *Far* is followed by *from*, not *of*, when the place in question is mentioned.

No vive lejos de Londres.	⊗He doesn't live far of London.⊗ He doesn't live far FROM London.
Te enseñaré cómo ir; no está lejos.	I'll show you the way – it's not FAR.

(2) It is not normally used in affirmative sentences: we prefer to say *a long way*.

Newcastle está lejos de Dover.	⊗Newcastle is far from Dover.⊗ (unusual) Newcastle is A LONG WAY FROM Dover.

Fathers

Fathers means *two men with children*: everyone has only one father! A person's father and mother are his *parents*.

Pediré permiso a mis padres.	⊗I'll ask my fathers for permission.⊗ I'll ask my PARENTS for permission.
Sus padres (el de John y el de Peter) trabajan juntos.	Their FATHERS (John's and Peter's) work together.

Fault

Fault has 2 common meanings.

(1) A personal failing('fallo'), something we don't like about a person.

La tozudez es uno de mis mayores defectos.	Stubbornness is one of my biggest FAULTS.

(2) When we blame someone for something. ('echar la culpa a alguién').

¡Vamos a llegar tarde y es culpa tuya!	We're going to be late, and it's all your FAULT!

(3) It is not the translation of 'falta' in the context of school work, for example, for this we use *mistake*.

En mi redacción hay muchas faltas.	⊗There are a lot of faults in my composition.⊗ There are a lot of MISTAKES in my composition.

Few, a few

Few means *not many*, is used with plural nouns only (or as a pronoun), and has a negative connotation.
A few is also used with plural nouns or as a pronoun, but means *some, more than one or two*. See also LITTLE/A LITTLE.

Tengo muy poco dinero.	⊗I have very few money.⊗ I have very LITTLE money. (I HAVEN'T VERY MUCH money).
Es una persona desagradable, por eso tiene pocos amigos.	⊗He is a very unpleasant person, so he has a few friends.⊗ He is a very unpleasant person so he has FEW friends. (so he HASN'T MANY friends).
Vi a algunas personas esperando delante del cine.	⊗I saw few people waiting outside the cinema.⊗ I saw A FEW/SOME people waiting outside the cinema.

To find

You *find* someone/something that has been lost or missing; you *meet* someone in the street/at the station etc..

El otro día encontré a un viejo amigo.	⊗I found an old friend the other day.⊗ I MET an old friend the other day.
Te recogeré en el aeropuerto.	⊗I'll find you at the airport.⊗ I'll MEET you at the airport.
¡Encontró a su hijo hablando con la chica de la caja!	She FOUND her son talking to the girl at the checkout!

To fit

An item of clothing *fits* you if it is the right size. Something *suits* you if you look good in it, if it's a nice colour etc..

–¿Me queda bien este vestido? *–Sí, te sienta muy bien.*	⊗"Do you think this dress fits me?"⊗ "Do you think this dress SUITS me?" "Yes, it looks lovely on you."
El otro jersey te quedaba pequeño, pero ésta te va bien/es tu talla.	⊗The other pullover was too small, but this one suits you.⊗ The other pullover was too small, but this one FITS you.

Floor

(1) *Floor* is used for indoors only; for outside, we use *ground*.

Se le cayó la cartera al suelo delante del cine. — ⊗He dropped his wallet on the floor outside the cinema.⊗

He dropped his wallet on the GROUND outside the cinema.

El suelo estaba cubierto de una preciosa moqueta blanca. — The FLOOR was covered by a beautiful white carpet.

(2) A person lives *on* the second/third *floor* of a building etc.

Vive en el sexto piso. — ⊗He lives in the sixth floor.⊗

He lives ON the sixth floor.

To follow

We say *to follow* a person/a direction/a course but with an action, we say to *continue* doing or to *go on* doing.

Siguieron jugando a pesar de la lluvia. — ⊗They followed playing in spite of the rain.⊗

They WENT ON/CONTINUED playing in spite of the rain.

Sigo el curso de alemán por la tele. — I'm FOLLOWING the German course on TV.

No te puedes perder: simplemente sigue las indicaciones. — You can't get lost – just FOLLOW the signs.

For

(1) *For* is used to say how long an action takes or lasts. It is often confused with *during* and with *since* when the Present Perfect tense is used. See DURING and SINCE.

(2) To express somebody's purpose ('propósito'), we can use *for* with a noun but not with a verb (whether in infinitive or '–ing' form): here we must use *to* with the infinitive form of the verb.

Paró para tomar algo. — ⊗He stopped for have a drink.⊗

⊗He stopped for to have a drink.⊗

He stopped TO HAVE a drink.

(He stopped FOR A drink)

Voy a clase para aprender inglés. — ⊗I go to class for learning English.⊗

I go to class TO LEARN English.

(3) But note that *for* can be used with the '–ing' form of a verb to express the purpose of an object (what something is used for).

Ese instrumento sirve para medir la presión atmosférica. — That instrument is used FOR MEASURING atmospheric pressure.

(4) In passive sentences, the preposition used with the agent is *by*, not *for*.

Kennedy fue asesinado por Lee Harvey Oswald en 1963. — ⊗Kennedy was assassinated for Lee Harvey Oswald in 1963.⊗

Kennedy was assassinated BY Lee Harvey Oswald in 1963.

Foreign, foreigner

Foreign is an adjective; *foreigner* is a noun, meaning *a foreign person*.

El Ministerio de Asuntos Exteriores.	⊗The Ministry of Foreigner Affairs.⊗ The Ministry of FOREIGN Affairs.
Es extranjero, pero vive aquí.	⊗He's a foreign, but he lives here.⊗ He's a FOREIGNER, but he lives here.

To forget

We do not use *to forget* if we say the place: in this case, we must use *to leave*.

Olvidó sus llaves en el despacho.	⊗He forgot his keys at the office.⊗ He LEFT his keys at the office.
He olvidado (traer) mi tarjeta VISA.	I've FORGOTTEN (to bring) my VISA card.

(In) front (of)

(1) *In front of* is the opposite of *behind*; we do not use it to refer to buildings, or to people or things on the other side of a room, street etc.

Quedamos delante del cine a las 8, ¿vale?	⊗I'll meet you in front of the cinema at 8.00, o.k.?⊗ I'll meet you OUTSIDE the cinema at 8.00, o.k.?
Hay un bar justo enfrente de mi casa.	⊗There is a bar just in front of my house.⊗ There is a bar just OPPOSITE my house.
Sólo había 3 personas delante de mí en la cola.	There were only 3 people IN FRONT OF me in the queue.

(2) Notice that *in front of* relates someone's position directly to that of another person or thing; but we say *at the front (or back)* of a cinema, theatre, bus, train etc., and *in the front (or back)* of a car.

No me gusta sentarme en la parte delantera de un autocar porque me pongo nervioso.	⊗I don't like sitting in the front of a coach; I feel nervous.⊗ I don't like sitting AT the front of a coach; I feel nervous.
Prefiero sentarme en las últimas filas del cine para no estar demasiado cerca de la pantalla.	⊗I prefer to sit in the back of the cinema so the screen isn't too close.⊗ I prefer to sit AT the back of the cinema so the screen isn't too close.
Subieron al coche: uno delante, dos detrás.	They got into the car, one IN the front, two IN the back.

Funny See also AMUSING

Funny means *comic*, something that makes you laugh. (It can also mean *strange* or *unusual* – see RARE). It does not translate 'divertido' when talking about a situation which is not comic: instead, we use *entertaining* or *enjoyable*.

La fiesta fue muy divertida.	⊗The party was very funny.⊗ The party was very ENJOYABLE. (I really ENJOYED the party).
La película de los hermanos Marx era muy divertida (me hizo reír mucho).	The Marx Brothers film was very FUNNY.

G

To get down See TRANSPORT

To get up See TRANSPORT

To go See TO COME

To go out

(1) You *go out* to the cinema, a pub etc. If you go to another town, e.g. for the weekend, you *go away*.

Ha salido fuera el fin de semana.	⊗He has gone out for the weekend.⊗ He has gone AWAY for the weekend.

(2) To translate 'salir', we normally use *to go out* only when the place is not mentioned; if it is mentioned, we use *to leave*.

Salió de su despacho a las 5.	⊗He went out from/of his office at 5 p.m.⊗ He LEFT his office at 5 p.m.
Se puso la chaqueta y salió (se marchó).	He put his jacket on and WENT OUT.

To grow

To grow can be used both transitively, i.e. with an object (*to grow flowers*), and intransitively, when it means *to increase in size*. *To grow up* is only used for the process of children getting older and becoming adults.

Este año cultivamos todo tipo de legumbres en el jardín.	This year, we're GROWING all sorts of vegetables in the garden.
Mi hijo ha crecido 7 cm en 6 meses.	⊗My son has grown up 3 inches in 6 months.⊗ My son has GROWN 3 inches in 6 months.
Esas plantas han crecido muy rápido.	⊗Those plants have grown up very fast.⊗ Those plants have GROWN very fast.
Es fascinante ver a tus propios hijos hacerse mayores.	It's fascinating to watch your children GROWING UP.

H

Hand, on the other

This expression is used to indicate contrast between 2 or more aspects of a situation – e.g. when talking about the advantages and disadvantages of something. It is not the translation of 'por otra parte' when the element of contrast is missing.

Ir en avión es la forma más rápida de viajar. Además/Por otra parte, es cómodo.	⊗Flying is the fastest way to travel. On the other hand, it is comfortable.⊗ Flying is the fastest way to travel. IN ADDITION, it is comfortable. (It is ALSO comfortable.)
Viajar en avión es muy cómodo, en cambio, puede ser peligroso.	Flying is very comfortable. ON THE OTHER HAND/HOWEVER, it can be dangerous.

Hardly

(1) *Hardly* means *almost not* and is translated by 'apenas'. The adverbial form of the adjective *hard* is also *hard.*

Ella trabaja duro.	⊗She works very hardly.⊗ She works very HARD.
Apenas ha estudiado este año.	He has HARDLY studied this year.

(2) *Hardly anybody/hardly anything* are used much more frequently than *almost nobody/almost nothing* etc.,

Casi nadie vio el accidente.	⊗Almost nobody saw the accident. (unusual)⊗ HARDLY ANYBODY saw the accident.

To have

(1) In modern British English, *to have* is used as a principal verb in 2 ways.

(a) When it has the meaning of possession or relationship (e.g. family), the negative and interrogative forms in the present tense are formed without the auxiliary verb *do*. We normally use *got* for all forms of the verb – affirmative, negative and interrogative.

¿Tienes coche?	⊗Do you have a car?⊗ (American English) HAVE YOU GOT a car?
No tengo hermanas pero sí dos hermanos.	⊗I don't have any sisters but I have 2 brothers.⊗ (American English) I HAVEN'T GOT any sisters but I've got (I have) 2 brothers.

(b) *To have* is used with many expressions without the meaning of possession, where it could be replaced by one of several other verbs, e.g. *to have a cup of coffee* (= to drink); *to have a shower* (= to wash oneself) etc. In these cases, *to have* is exactly like any other normal verb, i.e. it forms the negative and interrogative with the auxiliary verb *do*, and *got* is not used.

¿Tomas un baño cada noche?	⊗Have you (got) a bath every night?⊗ DO YOU HAVE a bath every night?
¿Qué tomas para desayunar?	What DO YOU HAVE for breakfast?

(2) In the past, the negative and interrogative forms for both uses of the verb (a) and (b) are normally with *did(n't)*. The interrogative form *Had you . . .?* is uncommon for group (a) and impossible for group (b).

¿Tenías muchos amigos cuando ibas al colegio?	⊗Had you many friends at school?⊗ (not common) DID YOU HAVE many friends at school?
No tomé café esta mañana.	⊗I hadn't a coffee this morning.⊗ I DIDN'T HAVE a coffee this morning.
No tenían mucho dinero cuando eran jovenes.	They DIDN'T HAVE much money (or: They HADN'T GOT much money) when they were young.

(3) *To have* is not used for people's ages – see AGE. See also COLD and HOT.
(4) Parts of the verb *to have* are often incorrectly used to translate 'hay/había' etc. (there is/are, there was/were).

Había un letrero que decía 'prohibido entrar'.	⊗It had a sign saying "No Entry".⊗ THERE WAS a sign saying "No Entry".
Hay mucha gente en el andén.	⊗They are/have a lot of people on the platform.⊗ THERE ARE a lot of people on the platform.

To hire See also TO LET, TO RENT

To hire is often confused with *to rent* and *to let*. You hire things generally for a short period of time – e.g. a car/boat/dinner-jacket ('un smoking'). You cannot *hire* a house or flat; for this, we use *to rent*, and also for things like televisions and video recorders. (It is also possible to *rent* a car – this is American English but is now widely used in Britain too.)

Alquilaron un chalet para el verano.	⊗They hired a villa for the summer.⊗ They RENTED a villa for the summer.
–No tengo smoking.	"I haven't got a dinner-jacket."
–¿Por qué no alquilas uno?	⊗"Why don't you rent one?"⊗ "Why don't you HIRE one?"

History

History refers to the study of the past: 'una historia' is a *story* (normally used with the verb *to tell*).

Nos contó una historia muy divertida.	⊗He told us a very funny history.⊗ He told us a very funny STORY.
La historia del siglo XIX es fascinante.	The HISTORY of the 19th century is fascinating.

Holiday

A *holiday* can be just one day or a longer period, though for longer periods we normally use the plural *holidays*. However, only the singular is used in expressions like *to go on holiday* or *to be on holiday*.

Se van de vacaciones la semana que viene.	⊗They are going on holidays next week.⊗
	They are going ON HOLIDAY next week.
El próximo jueves es fiesta.	⊗Next Thursday is holiday.⊗
	Next Thursday is A HOLIDAY.
Disfrutaron mucho de sus vacaciones.	They really enjoyed their HOLIDAY(S).

Home

The only preposition used with *home* is *at*, meaning *in one's house*, when there is no movement. With verbs of motion, no preposition is used.

Voy a casa ahora.	⊗I am going to home now.⊗
	I am going HOME now.
Está en casa, estudiando.	⊗He is in home, studying.⊗
	He is AT home, studying.
Llegaron tarde a casa.	⊗They arrived to/at home late.⊗
	They arrived HOME late.

To hope

(1) See TO EXPECT.
(2) It must be followed by *for* when used with a direct object.

Espero que me contèsten pronto.	⊗I am hoping a reply soon.⊗
	I am hoping FOR a reply soon.

Hot

Hot is an extreme of temperature: *warm* is more moderate (see COLD).

Incluso en invierno, cuando sale el sol, la temperatura puede ser agradable.	⊗Even in winter it can be hot when the sun comes out.⊗
	Even in winter it can be WARM when the sun comes out.
En el desierto hace muchísimo calor de día.	In the desert, it is extremely HOT during the day.
Llévate ropa de abrigo por si hace frío luego.	⊗Take hot clothes with you in case it is cold later on.⊗
	Take WARM clothes with you in case it is cold later on.

How

(1) *How* is often confused with *as* and *like*: it is only used in direct or

indirect questions, and not in comparisons (see also AS and LIKE). It is not normally placed at the beginning of a sentence.

Como sabes, se casaron el año pasado.	⊗How you know, they got married last year.⊗
	AS you know, they got married last year.
Busca un buen trabajo, como todo el mundo.	⊗He's looking for a good job, how everybody else.⊗
	He's looking for a good job, LIKE everybody else.
Díme cómo te fue.	Tell me HOW you got on.

(2) *How* is not normally used after a verb of perception (most commonly *to see* or *to watch*) where 'como' followed by a past tense is used in Spanish.

Vieron como un tipo sacaba una pistola y empezaba a disparar.	⊗They saw how a man pulled out a gun and began to shoot.⊗
	They saw A MAN PULL OUT a gun and BEGIN to shoot.

How?

(1) We use *How*? with the verb *to be* to ask about someone's health.

–¿Cómo está tu madre?	"HOW is your mother?"
–Muy bien, gracias.	"Oh, fine, thanks."

(2) To ask about the appearance of a place or someone's character, we must use *what . . . . like*?, also with the verb *to be.*

–¿Cómo son las islas griegas?	⊗"How are the Greek islands?"⊗
	"WHAT are the Greek islands LIKE?"
–¿Cómo es tu hermana?	⊗"How is your sister (like)"⊗
–Bueno, es rubia y un poco más alta que yo.	"WHAT is your sister LIKE?"
	"Well, she's blond and a bit taller than me."

(3) In current colloquial English, it is becoming more common in the past tense only to ask questions with *How*? instead of *What . . . like*?, but not everybody accepts this as being correct.

–¿Cómo te fue el examen?	"WHAT was your exam LIKE?" (or "HOW was your exam?")

How long?

(1) *How long*? is not followed by *time*.

¿Cuánto tardas en ir al trabajo?	⊗How long time/How much time do you take to get to work?⊗
	HOW LONG do you take/does it take you to get work?

(2) It is commonly used with the Present Perfect tense in English where Spanish uses a Present tense.

¿Cuánto hace que vives aquí?	⊗How long are you living here?⊗ HOW LONG HAVE YOU BEEN LIVING here?

(3) It is not used for distance: for this, we use *How far*?.

¿A qué distancia está Bonn de Berlin?	⊗How long is Bonn from Berlin?⊗ How FAR is Bonn from Berlin?

I

If

(1) *If* clauses: the tenses used in if clauses in English correspond in almost every case to the Spanish tense (although English does not use the subjunctive, with rare exceptions). The most common error is to use the same tense of the verb in the *if* clause as in the main clause. See below for the 3 main types of *if* sentence.

Te llamaré mañana si tengo tiempo.	⊗I'll give you a ring tomorrow if I will have time.⊗
	I'll give you a ring tomorrow if I HAVE time.
Si tuviese suficiente dinero, me compraría un coche nuevo.	⊗If I would have enough money I would buy a new car.⊗
	If I HAD enough money, I would buy a new car.
	(I'd buy a new car).
Si me lo hubieras dicho antes podría haberte ayudado.	⊗If you would have told me earlier, I could have helped you.⊗
	If you HAD told me earlier, I could have helped you.

(2a) In reported speech, *if* and *whether* can both be used to introduce questions which have no question word (e.g. *who*?, *when*?) but *whether* is more common when two possible alternatives are mentioned.

Preguntó si estaban listos para salir.	He asked IF/WHETHER they were ready to leave.
Hazme saber si puedes venir.	Let me know WHETHER you can come or not. (IF is also possible but not as common)

(2b) *If* cannot be used after a preposition or before an infinitive.

No sé si salir o quedarme en casa.	⊗I don't know if to go out or stay at home.⊗
	I don't know WHETHER to go out or stay at home.

Hablaron sobre si deberían comprar la casa o no. — ⊗They talked about if to buy the house or not.⊗

They talked about WHETHER to buy the house or not.

To ignore

To ignore means *not to pay attention to* or *not to say hello to somebody*: it does not have the meaning of *not to know*.

No me hizo caso en toda la noche. — She IGNORED me all night.

Ignoro/no sé por qué nunca sale. — ⊗I ignore why he never goes out.⊗

I DON'T KNOW why he never goes out.

Ill

Ill and *sick* are very similar but:

(1) *Ill* generally implies something more serious than *sick*.

Su padre está muy grave. — His father is extremely ILL.

(2) *Sick* is used when the sense is *to vomit*.

Varios invitados vomitaron después de comer mejillones. — Several of the guests were SICK after eating mussels.

(3) *Ill* is not used before a noun or as a collective adjective.

Está muy enferma. — ⊗She's a very ill woman.⊗

She's very ILL.

Quería ser enfermera para cuidar a los enfermos. — ⊗She wanted to be a nurse to look after the ill.⊗

She wanted to be a nurse to look after the SICK.

Illusion

To have illusions in English means *to have a false impression* or *to have a distorted vision of reality*. To translate 'tener ilusión', we use a variety of expressions – a common one is *to look forward to*.

Este viaje me hace mucha ilusión. — ⊗I have a lot of illusion about the trip.⊗

I'M (REALLY) LOOKING FORWARD TO the trip.

Creyeron ver un lago, pero fue un espejismo. — They thought they could see a lake, but it was just an ILLUSION.

Important See also IMPRESSIVE

This adjective means *to have importance* in a positive sense and is therefore not used to describe e.g. an injury or accident.

Tenía un corte importante en la cabeza. — ⊗He had an important cut on his head.⊗

He had a SERIOUS cut on his head.

Esta tarde tengo una reunión importante. — I have an IMPORTANT meeting this afternoon.

Impressive See also IMPORTANT

Impressive always has a positive sense and therefore cannot be used to describe a fire/an accident/a natural disaster etc..

Ayer hubo un impresionante accidente en el centro de la ciudad.	⊗There was an impressive accident in the city centre yesterday.⊗
	There was a SERIOUS/TERRIBLE accident in the city centre yesterday.
El actor hizo un papel impresionante.	The actor gave a very IMPRESSIVE performance.

To intend

To intend (to do) means *to have the intention*, not *to try*.

Intentaron subir al Everest pero tuvieron que abandonar a causa del mal tiempo.	⊗They intended to climb Everest but had to give up because of the bad weather.⊗
	They TRIED to climb Everest but had to give up because of the bad weather.
Tengo la intención de montar un negocio dentro de poco.	I INTEND to begin a business soon.

To interview

Interview can be both a verb and a noun. The correct uses are:
(a) as a verb, *to interview someone*.
(b) as a noun, *to have an interview with someone*.

Le hicieron una entrevista.	⊗They made him an interview.⊗
	⊗They interviewed to/with him.⊗
	They INTERVIEWED him.
Se entrevistó con su jefe.	⊗He did an interview with his boss.⊗
	He HAD an interview with his boss.

In/into

(1) We use *in* for a position without movement.

Había 3 personas en la habitación.	⊗There were 3 people into the room.⊗
	There were 3 people IN the room.

(2) *Into* is used instead of *in* when there is a verb of movement and it is followed by a place.

Entró en el despacho.	⊗He walked in the office.⊗
	He walked INTO the office.
Abrió la puerta y entró.	⊗He opened the door and went into.⊗
	He opened the door and went IN.
¡Adelante! (¡Pase!)	⊗Come into!⊗
	Come IN!

To invite

In English, we *invite* someone to a party or some part of celebration but we say *to pay for* or *to stand (someone)* a meal or a drink etc. when we mean *to pay for oneself and for another person*.

Invito yo.	⊗I invite you.⊗ I'll PAY FOR this/I'll STAND (you) this one.
Fuimos a cenar y me invitaron mis alumnos.	⊗We went out for dinner, and my students invited me.⊗ (This means: 'Mis alumnos me invitaron a que fuera con ellos'.) We went out for dinner, and my students PAID FOR ME.
Fui invitado a la boda.	I was INVITED to the wedding.

J

Journey

See also TO TRAVEL

Journey and *trip* are often confused: *journey* usually refers to the movement to or from the place visited; *trip* usually refers to the movement and the stay together.

Acorte su viaje: ¡Coja el tren!	⊗Cut your trip time – take the train!⊗ Cut your JOURNEY time – take the train!
–¿Cómo te fue el viaje (de negocios)?	⊗"How did your (business) journey go?"⊗ "How did your (business) TRIP go?"
–Un éxito, gracias.	"Oh, it was successful, thanks."

K

To know

(1) *To know* cannot be used for an action which takes place at one specific moment. We say *to meet* a person for the first time; then, very often there is a period when you *get to know* that person; finally, you can claim to *know* the person. For news, information etc. we say *to find out/to hear* etc..

Lo conocí en una fiesta.	⊗I knew him at a party.⊗ I MET him at a party.
Tardé mucho en conocerla.	⊗It took me a long time to know her.⊗ It took me a long time to GET TO KNOW her.
Claro que le conozco: nos conocimos el año pasado.	Yes, of course I KNOW him: we MET last year.
Supe la noticia por la radio.	⊗I knew the news on the radio.⊗ I HEARD the news on the radio.

(2) Notice that we can use *get to know* for a country but it is unusual to use *know* – we prefer to say *been to.*

¿Conoces Escocia?	⊗Do you know Scotland?⊗ (unusual) HAVE YOU (EVER) BEEN TO Scotland?
He estado muchas veces en la India: cuanto más la conozco mas me gusta.	I've been to India many times: the more I GET TO KNOW it, the more I love it.

Known

We say that a person or place is *famous* or *well-known*. *Known* is not used on its own in this context.

Es un actor muy conocido.	⊗He is a very known actor.⊗ He is a very WELL-KNOWN/FAMOUS actor.
Esta plaza es muy conocida a causa de la revolución.	⊗This square is very known because of the revolution.⊗ This square is WELL-KNOWN/FAMOUS because of the revolution.

L

Large

Large means *big*, not *long*.

Es una carretera muy larga.	⊗It's a very large road.⊗ It's a very LONG road.
La ballena es el mamífero más grande del mundo.	The whale is the LARGEST mammal in the world.

Last

(1) *Last* is often confused with *latest*, which means *the most recent*, *the newest*; *last* means *the last of a series* or *the one before this one*.

Me gusta mucho el último album de los Rollings (el más nuevo).	⊗I really like the Stones' last album.⊗ I really like the Stones' LATEST album.

¿Has visto la última moda en pantalones? — ⊗Have you seen the last fashion in trousers?⊗
Have you seen the LATEST fashion in trousers?

'Let It Be' fue el último album de los Beatles. — 'Let It Be' was the Beatles' LAST album.

Su última novela es mucho mejor que la anterior. — His LATEST novel is much better than his LAST one.

(2) We say *the last* when we mean *the final one of a series* or when we talk about a period that continues up to the present moment: but we say *last* without *the* when talking about *the one before this one*, usually a month/week/year.

El año pasado fui a Egipto. — ⊗The last year, I went to Egypt.⊗
LAST year, I went to Egypt.

Este último año ha sido un gran éxito. — THE LAST year has been very successful. (The 12 months up to now.)

Diciembre es el último mes del año. — December is THE LAST month of the year.

To lay

It is very easy to confuse *to lay* with *to lie.*
To lay is a transitive verb, i.e. it has an object. It is a regular verb (past form *laid*); the participle form is *laying*.
To lie is intransitive – it cannot have an object – and is irregular (past forms *lay, lain*). The participle form is *lying*. (Note that the regular verb *lie/lied/lied* means 'mentir'.)

Estaban tumbados en la playa. — ⊗They were laying on the beach.⊗
They were LYING on the beach.

Estoy cansado, voy a tumbarme. — ⊗I'm tired, I'm going to lay down.⊗
I'm tired, I'm going to LIE down.

El libro estaba en la mesa. — ⊗The book laid on the table.⊗
The book LAY on the table.

¿Quieres poner la mesa? — Will you LAY the table, please?

To lend See TO BORROW

To let

(1) *Let* is the translation of 'dejar' only when the sense is *to allow. To* is not used with it when it is followed by a verb.

Mis padres no me dejan volver a casa muy tarde. — ⊗My parents won't let me to stay out late.⊗
My parents won't LET me STAY out late.

(2) In other contexts, 'dejar' is usually translated by *to leave* in the sense of *to forget* or *to go to another place*.

He olvidado mi libro en casa.

⊗I've let my book at home.⊗

I've LEFT my book at home.

(3) We say *to lend* when we mean *to give an object for a short time.*

¿Me dejas tu bolígrafo?

⊗Can you let/leave me your pen?⊗

Can you LEND me your pen?

To lie

(1) See TO LAY.

Singapur se encuentra casi en el Ecuador.

Singapore LIES almost on the Equator.

(2) Remember that there are two verbs with this infinitive: to *lie/lay/lain* ('tumbarse', 'yacer') and *to lie/lied/lied* ('mentir'). The participle for both verbs is *lying*.

Mintió a la policía para proteger a sus cómplices.

He LIED to the police to protect his accomplices.

Like

(1) *Like* is often confused with *as*. The basic difference is *like* is a preposition and is followed by a noun or pronoun, but not by a verb or adverb; *as* is a conjunction and is followed by a subject and verb, or by a prepositional expression.

Trabajo en una fábrica, como mi padre.

⊗I work in a factory, like my father does.⊗

I work in a factory, LIKE my FATHER (or: AS my father DOES.)

En 1986, como en 1978, Argentina ganó el campeonato del mundo.

⊗In 1986, like in 1978, Argentina won the World Cup.⊗

In 1986, AS in 1978, Argentina won the World Cup.

Llega tarde, como siempre.

⊗Like always, he's late!⊗

AS always, he's late!

(2) With the verb *to work*, we use *as* to talk about the job or profession, and *like* simply to make a comparison.

Trabaja como periodista.

⊗She works like a journalist.⊗

She works AS a journalist.

Trabajó como un esclavo.

⊗He worked as a slave.⊗

He worked LIKE a slave.

(3) There are a number of verbs followed by a construction with *as*, not *like*. Among the most common are: to accept, to be known, to describe, to regard, to use.

Lo aceptaron enseguida como a uno de la familia.

⊗They accepted him like one of the family immediately.⊗

They accepted him AS one of the family immediately.

Se le conoce como 'el viejo maestro'. — ⊗He is known like 'the Old Maestro'.⊗ He is known AS 'the Old Maestro'.

N.B. In modern conversational English, it is becoming more common to use *like* with a subject and verb, e.g. *I hope it's a great summer* LIKE *we had 2 years ago*, but many people consider this incorrect.

To like

See also TO ENJOY

(1) *To like* is normally followed by the '-ing' form of a verb when the meaning is *to enjoy an activity*.

Me gusta esquiar en invierno y hacer windsurf en verano. — ⊗I like ski in winter and windsurf in summer.⊗

I LIKE SKIING in winter and WINDSURFING in summer.

(2) It can be used with the infinitive when the meaning is *I am in the habit of . . .* or *I think it is a good thing to. . . .*

Me gusta tomar un baño justo antes de acostarme: me relaja. — ⊗I like have a bath just before going to bed: it relaxes me.⊗

I LIKE TO HAVE (or HAVING) a bath just before going to bed: it relaxes me.

(3) The conditional form *would like* must be followed by an infinitive and refers to this moment. *Do you like*? is a more general question about somebody's tastes etc..

¿Te apetece salir a tomar algo? — ⊗Would you like going out for a drink?⊗

Would you LIKE TO GO out for a drink?

¿Quieres un trozo de pastel? — ⊗Do you like a piece of cake?⊗

WOULD you LIKE a piece of cake?

¿Te gusta el chocolate? — DO YOU LIKE chocolate?

(4) A person can like a thing but not vice-versa.

Me gustó mucho la película. — ⊗The film liked me very much.⊗

⊗I liked very much the film.⊗

I LIKED THE FILM very much.

(5) *To like* must be followed by an object. When using *very much*, the object must immediately follow *to like*.

–La semana pasada éstuve en París. — 'I was in Paris last week.'

–¿Te gustó? — ⊗'Did you like?'⊗

'Did you LIKE IT?'

Me gusta mucho bailar. — ⊗I like very much dancing.⊗

I LIKE DANCING VERY MUCH.

To listen

(1) When it is followed by a noun or pronoun, we must use *to* with the verb *to listen*.

Me gusta escuchar música. — ⊗I like listening music.⊗

I like LISTENING TO music.

¡Escucha! ¡Hay alguien fuera!	LISTEN! There's someone outside!

(2) The verb implies a wish or an effort to hear someone or something; if the action is involuntary, we must use the verb *to hear.*

Podía oír el tráfico en la calle.	⊗I could listen to the traffic in the street.⊗ I could HEAR the traffic in the street.

Little/a little

Little used as an adjective of quantity means *not much*, is used with uncountable nouns only, and has a negative connotation.
A little is also used with uncountable nouns only but means *a small quantity/amount of*, *some*, i.e. a more positive meaning. See also FEW/A FEW.

Era muy temprano y vi a muy poca gente en la calle.	⊗It was very early, and I saw very little people in the street.⊗ It was very early, and I saw very FEW people in the street. (or: I DIDN'T see very MANY people in the street.)
Compramos muy poca carne porque ¡es tan cara!	⊗We buy a little meat because it's so expensive.⊗ We buy LITTLE meat (or: We DON'T buy MUCH meat) because it's so expensive.
¿Te apetece un poco de queso?	⊗Would you like little cheese?⊗ Would you like A LITTLE cheese?

Lonely   See ALONE

To look   See TO SEEM

To look forward to

This verb means *to anticipate with pleasure*, to think about something pleasant you are going to do. It is followed by a noun or a verb in the '–ing' form, not the infinitive (the *to* is a preposition which forms part of this verb: it does not belong to the verb which follows). In conversation or informal style, we normally use the continuous form of the verb: *I look forward to* is much more formal – for example, in a business letter.

Tiene muchas ganas de conocerte.	⊗He is looking forward to meet you.⊗ He is looking forward to MEETING you.
Estas vacaciones me hacen mucha ilusión.	⊗I look forward to my holidays.⊗ (this would mean always or every year). I'M LOOKING forward to my holidays. (specific holidays)
Esperamos tener noticias suyas en un futuro próximo.	We LOOK forward to hearing from you in the near future. (at the end of a formal letter)

To lose

(1) *To lose* is not used with transport – we say *to miss* the bus/train etc.

Si no te das prisa perderás el tren.	⊗If you don't hurry, you will lose the train.⊗
	If you don't hurry, you will MISS the train.

(2) If you spend time badly, you *waste* time, not *lose* time.

Perdió todo el día: no hizo nada.	⊗He lost the whole day, doing nothing.⊗
	He WASTED the whole day, doing nothing.

Luck

Luck is a noun. The adjectival form is *lucky*, used with the verb *to be*.

¡Siempre tiene suerte!	⊗He always has luck/lucky.⊗
	He IS always LUCKY!

M

To make

(1) See TO DO (group 4). See below for some of the most common expressions with *to make*.

equivocarse	⊗to do a mistake⊗
	to MAKE a mistake
tomar una decisión	to MAKE a decision
hacer una oferta	to MAKE an offer
sugerir/proponer	to MAKE a suggestion
hacer una llamada	to MAKE a phone call
hacer un esfuerzo	to MAKE an effort
hacer planes	to MAKE plans
ganar dinero	to MAKE money
hacer el amor/la guerra	to MAKE love/war
hacer la cama	to MAKE the bed
hacer ruido	to MAKE noise

(2) With the meaning of *to force* or *to oblige*, we say *to make someone do something*: it is not followed by *to*, except in the passive.

Los atracadores obligaron al director a entregar el dinero.	⊗The bank robbers made the manager to hand over the money.⊗
	The bank robbers MADE the manager HAND OVER the money.
El director fue obligado a entregar el dinero.	The manager was MADE TO HAND OVER the money.

Many

(1) *Many* is only used with plural nouns.

No tengo mucho dinero.	⊗I haven't got many money.⊗ I haven't got MUCH money.

(2) It is uncommon in the affirmative, where we prefer to use *a lot of*. (See also MUCH)

Tiene muchos amigos.	⊗She has many friends.⊗ (uncommon). She has A LOT OF friends.

Mark

We talk about *marks* in an exam (see NOTE) but 'la marca', referring to a product, is the *make* or *model*.

¿De qué marca es tu radio?	⊗What mark is your radio?⊗ What MAKE is your radio?
–¿Qué nota sacaste? *–Siete.*	"What MARK did you get?" "7".

To marry

(1) *To marry* is used with a direct object (in normal spoken English) and without a preposition.

Se casó con un príncipe.	⊗She married with a prince.⊗ She MARRIED a prince.

(2) If there is no direct object, we prefer to use *to get married*.

Se casaron el año pasado.	⊗They married last year.⊗ (uncommon) They GOT MARRIED last year.

(3) If we use *to get married* with an object, the preposition is *to* and not *with*. (Similarly with *to be married*.)

Se casó con su prima.	⊗He got married with his cousin.⊗ He got MARRIED TO his cousin.
Está casado con una italiana.	⊗He is married with an Italian girl.⊗ He is MARRIED TO an Italian girl.

To matter

(1) *To matter* is most often used in the impersonal form negative – *it doesn't matter*, meaning *it is not important*.

–Está lloviendo. *–No importa, voy a salir igual.*	"It's raining." ⊗"Doesn't matter, I'm still going out."⊗ "IT doesn't matter, I'm still going out."

(2) It can, of course, also be used with specific subjects, which must come before the verb.

Sus opiniones no cuentan para nada.

⊗Don't matter his opinions.⊗

His opinions DON'T MATTER.

(3) The translation of 'no te preocupes' is *don't worry*, not *don't matter*.

-Aún no he escrito esa carta.
-Bueno, no te preocupes.

"I haven't written that letter yet."
⊗"Oh, don't matter."⊗
"Oh, don't WORRY (about it)."

May

See MODAL AUXILIARY VERBS, POSSIBLE

Me

Me is the object form of *I*, used as a direct/indirect object or after most prepositions, but it is not used after *of* in a possessive sense; for this, we must use both the preposition and the possessive form *mine*. (Similarly with object/possessive pronouns – *us/ours*, *him/his*, *them/theirs* etc.).

Es un buen amigo mío.

⊗He is a good friend of me.⊗
He is a good friend OF MINE.

¿Conoces a algún amigo suyo?

⊗Do you know any friends of them?⊗
Do you know any friends OF THEIRS?

To mean

The verb *to mean* is a normal verb used with *do* or *did* in present/past negative and interrogative forms.

¿Qué significa 'scared'?

⊗What means 'scared'?⊗
⊗What does mean 'scared'?⊗
What DOES 'scared' MEAN?

Meanwhile

Meanwhile is an adverb ('mientras tanto'); it is often confused with *while*, which is a conjunction ('mientras'). Only *while* can be followed by a clause.

Mientras hacía la compra en el supermercado, me robaron el monedero.

⊗Meanwhile I was shopping in the supermarket, I had my purse stolen.⊗
WHILE I was shopping in the supermarket, I had my purse stolen.

Uno de los detectives interrogó al sospechoso. Mientras tanto, su colega consultó las fichas.

One detective interrogated the suspect. MEANWHILE, his colleague looked through the files.

Might

See MODAL AUXILIARY VERBS, POSSIBLE

To mind

(1) *To mind* cannot be used impersonally – see MATTER.

No importa.	⊗It doesn't mind.⊗ It doesn't MATTER.

(2) It is normally used in negative and interrogative sentences. It means *to object to* or *to dislike* and therefore is used only with something which many people would dislike or find boring; it is not used for something normally considered interesting or pleasant, e.g. going on holiday.

¿Te molesta ir de vacaciones?	⊗Do you mind going on holiday?⊗ (Going on holiday is a PLEASANT idea for everybody.)

(3) It is never followed by the infinitive. The interrogative forms *Do you mind. . .?* and *Would you mind. . .?* can be followed by an if-clause or a verb in the '–ing' form, but not by the infinitive.

No me importa/molesta lavar los platos.	⊗I don't mind to wash the dishes.⊗ I don't mind WASHING the dishes.
¿Podría Vd. abrir la ventana?	⊗Would you mind to open the window?⊗ Would you mind OPENING the window?
¿Le importa que fume?	⊗Do you mind that I smoke?⊗ Do you mind IF I smoke?
¿Te molesta que la gente grite en la calle?	⊗Do you mind that people shout in the street?⊗ Do you mind people SHOUTING in the street?

(4) The translation of 'no te preocupes' is *don't worry* – see also MATTER.

–Aún no he acabado aquel trabajo.	"I haven't finished that work yet."
–Bueno, no te preocupes.	⊗"Well, don't mind."⊗ "Well, don't WORRY."

Mine

The pronoun form of the possessive adjective *my* is *mine*, not *the mine* or *the my one* (these forms do not exist). (Similarly for *yours*, *his*, *hers*, *ours* and *theirs*.)

Este libro es tuyo: ¿has visto el mío?	⊗This is your book: have you seen the mine/the my one?⊗ This is your book: have you seen MINE?

Modal auxiliary verbs

There are 4 common mistakes made with this group of verbs (principally *can*, *could*, *may*, *might*, *must*, *should*).
(1) Using *to* before the principal verb – the only modal verb which can be followed by *to* is *ought to*.

Todo el mundo tiene que pagar (sus) impuestos.

⊗Everybody must to pay taxes.⊗

Everybody MUST PAY taxes.

Pienso que deberías disculparte por haberte comportado así.

⊗I think you should to apologize for your behaviour.⊗

I think you SHOULD APOLOGIZE (or: you OUGHT TO APOLOGIZE) for your behaviour.

(2) Using them with the Simple Past form of the principal verb, instead of an infinitive form, to express the past.

Puede que se haya ido fuera el fin de semana.

⊗He might went away for the weekend.⊗

He MIGHT HAVE GONE away for the weekend.

Debía haber ido en coche, es más rápido.

⊗He should has/had gone by car, it's faster.⊗

He should HAVE gone by car, it's faster.

(3) Using them in the non-existent infinitive form.

Llegó temprano, para poder ver a su padre.

⊗He arrived early, to can see his father.⊗

He arrived early, TO BE ABLE to see (or: SO AS to see) his father.

(4) Using them with *do* or *did* in question or negative forms.

¿Sabes nadar?

⊗Do you can swim?⊗

CAN YOU SWIM?

Moment, at the

(1) *At* (not *in*) *the moment* means *now*, *currently*, *at present*.

Actualmente no trabaja.

⊗He's not working in this moment.⊗

He's not working AT THE MOMENT.

(2) To translate 'al momento', we use *at once/straight away/immediately*.

–No se preocupe señor, ahora mismo le traigo la sopa.

⊗"Don't worry, sir, I'll bring you your soup at the moment."⊗

"Don't worry, sir, I'll bring you your soup AT ONCE/STRAIGHT AWAY."

More

More is the comparative form of *much/many*.

(1) It cannot be used to express the superlative – for this, we use *most*.

Venecia es la ciudad más bonita que jamás he visto.

⊗Venice is the more beautiful city I've ever seen.⊗

Venice is the MOST beautiful city I've ever seen.

(2) It is not used to form the comparative of most adjectives of one or two syllables, but only for longer adjectives, when it must be followed by *than*, not *that*.

Este paquete es más pequeño que el otro.	⊗This packet is more small than the other one.⊗ This packet is SMALLER than the other one.
La gramática alemana es más difícil que la inglesa.	⊗German grammar is more difficult that English grammar.⊗ German grammar is more difficult THAN English grammar.

Most

(1) *Most* can only be preceded by *the* when used with an adjective in the superlative form. When the meaning of *most* is *the majority of*, followed by a noun (or adjective and noun), *the* cannot be used.

La mayoría de la gente está en contra de la guerra.	⊗The most people are against war.⊗ MOST people are against war.
Granada es una de las ciudades más bonitas de Europa.	Granada is one of THE MOST beautiful cities in Europe.

(2) When *the most* is used in the superlative sense, we must insert *thing* in English if there is no specific noun.

Lo más importante es comprobar la fecha en el billete.	⊗The most important is to check the date on the ticket.⊗ The most important THING is to check the date on the ticket.

(3) It can only be used with *of* before a noun when there is also a determiner (e.g. the, my, those etc.).

La mayoría de los médicos recomiendan no fumar.	⊗Most of doctors recommend people not to smoke.⊗ MOST DOCTORS recommend people not to smoke.
La mayoría de mis amigos están casados.	MOST OF MY friends are married.

Much

(1) *Much* is not common in affirmative sentences – we prefer to use *a lot (of)*.

Tengo mucho tiempo libre.	⊗I have much free time.⊗ (unusual) I have A LOT OF free time.

(2) It is only used with uncountable nouns – for plural nouns, we use *many*.

¿Viste a mucha gente en la ciudad?	⊗Did you see much people in town?⊗ Did you see MANY people in town?
Nos queda muy poco café.	We haven't (got) MUCH coffee left.

Must

(1) *Must* is never followed by *to* – see MODAL AUXILIARY VERBS. In the present, it can have two different meanings – obligation and deduction.

Tengo que irme: es muy tarde.	⊗I must to go: it's very late.⊗ I MUST go: it's very late. (obligation)
Tiene que ser rico – acaba de comprarse un Rolls.	⊗He must to be rich – he has just bought a Rolls-Royce.⊗ He MUST be rich – he has just bought a Rolls-Royce. (deduction)

(2) *Must* has no past form. To express obligation in the past, we use *had to*; to express deduction in the past, we use *must* with the Present Perfect form of the principal verb.

Tuvo que pagar una multa (por aparcar mal).	⊗He must paid/must had paid/must have pay a parking fine.⊗ He HAD TO PAY a parking fine. (obligation)
Sus abuelos deben haber sido muy interesantes.	⊗His grandparents must were/must had been interesting people.⊗ His grandparents MUST HAVE BEEN interesting people. (supposition – they are dead now)

(3) *Mustn't* is used for an obligation in the negative; to express a lack of obligation, we use *needn't* or *don't have to*; to express a supposition in the negative, we normally use *can't*.

No debes/no se puede aparcar en la acera.	You MUSTN'T park on the pavement. (negative obligation)
No tienes que venir si no te apetece.	⊗You mustn't come if you don't want to.⊗ You NEEDN'T COME if you don't want to. (or: you DON'T HAVE TO COME.) (lack of obligation)
No puede tener 20 años – hace sólo un año que dejó el colegio.	⊗He mustn't be 20 – he only left school last year.⊗ He CAN'T BE 20 – he only left school last year. (negative supposition)

N

Near

Near is a preposition only. It is not normally used with *to*.
Nearby is both the adverbial and adjectival form. N.B. *Close to* can be used instead of *near*.

Vive cerca de la iglesia.	⊗He lives near to the church.⊗ He lives NEAR the church. (or: He lives CLOSE TO the church.)
Había algunas tiendas cerca.	⊗There were some shops near.⊗ There were some shops NEARBY.
Durmieron en un pueblo cercano.	⊗They slept in a near village.⊗ They slept in a NEARBY village.

To need (present)

(1) The verb *to need* can be used as an ordinary verb and also as a modal auxiliary verb (nearly always in the negative in the present tense, when *needn't do* is an alternative to *don't need to do*).

Seguramente no necesitamos reservar asiento: el tren no estará lleno.	⊗I'm sure we needn't to book a seat: the train won't be full.⊗ I'm sure we NEEDN'T book a seat (or: I'm sure we DON'T NEED TO book a seat): the train won't be full.
Necesita echarse; no se encuentra bien.	⊗He needs lie down – he's not feeling well.⊗ He NEEDS TO lie down – he's not feeling well.

(2) *Needn't* cannot be used with a direct object.

No necesitas impermeable, hace sol.	⊗You needn't a raincoat: it's sunny.⊗ You DON'T NEED a raincoat: it's sunny.

To need (past)

The past forms *didn't need to do* and *needn't have done* have very different meanings. *Didn't need to* means that the subject knew that it wasn't necessary to do something and so didn't do it; *needn't have done* means that the subject did something and only later realised that it hadn't been necessary to do it.

No hacía falta que hubiera comprado café, ya que su esposa ya había comprado (pero, al no saberlo él, compró más).	⊗He didn't need to have bought coffee.⊗ (because his wife had already bought some) He NEEDN'T have bought coffee. (But he did buy some.)
No necesitó coger un taxi para ir a la estación, ya que le sobraba tiempo (sabía	⊗He needn't take a taxi to the station, as he had plenty of time.⊗

que tenía tiempo de sobras y no cogió un taxi.)	He DIDN'T NEED TO take a taxi to the station, as he had plenty of time. (He didn't take a taxi.)

Negatives

(1) In English it is not possible to use two negatives together in a sentence, so we eliminate either the negative part of the verb or the negative word used following the verb.

No vi a nadie.	⊗I didn't see nobody.⊗ I didn't see ANYBODY. (or: I SAW NOBODY.)
No pueden hacer nada.	⊗They can't do nothing.⊗ They can't do ANYTHING. (or: They CAN DO NOTHING.)

(2) When forming the negative of a normal verb in the present tense, the form of the principal verb does not change in the third person singular, when *doesn't* is used.

Ya no vive aquí.	⊗He doesn't lives here any more.⊗ He doesn't LIVE here any more.

(3) When forming the negative of a normal verb in the past, the principal verb is in the infinitive form (without *to*), not in the past form.

No salieron de casa hasta las 11.00.	⊗They didn't left home until 11.00.⊗ They didn't LEAVE home until 11.00.

Neither/nor

Neither or *Nor* mean also not and are used following, or in response to, a negative expression. They must come first in the expression. An auxiliary verb (or *to be*) must be used, in the affirmative form, and come before the subject. Alternatively, if we wish to respond by using a subject with a negative auxiliary verb (in the normal word order), we must follow this with *either*, not *neither*.

–No me gustan los lunes. *–A mí tampoco.*	"I don't like Mondays." ⊗"Neither like I."/"Neither I⊗ ⊗like."/"Neither I do."/⊗ ⊗"Neither don't I."/"I don't,⊗ ⊗neither."⊗ "Neither DO I." (or: "NOR DO I.") (or: "I DON'T, EITHER.")
–Él no es muy inteligente. *–Su hermana, tampoco.*	"He's not very intelligent." ⊗"Neither isn't his sister."/⊗ ⊗"Neither his sister is."/⊗ ⊗"His sister isn't, neither."⊗ "Neither IS HIS SISTER." (or: "NOR IS HIS SISTER.") (or: "His sister ISN'T, EITHER.")

–No salí anoche.	"I didn't go out last night."
–Yo tampoco.	⊗"Neither I didn't."/"Neither⊗ ⊗didn't I."/"I didn't,⊗ ⊗neither."⊗
	"Neither DID I." (or: "NOR DID I.") (or: "I DIDN'T, EITHER.")

Nervous

In English, you are *nervous* if you are worried about something, e.g. the day before an important exam; but you feel *angry* or *annoyed* if another person does or says something which you consider to be offensive or stupid.

Se puso muy nervioso cuando un coche chocó contra el suyo.	⊗He got very nervous when another car bumped his.⊗
	He got very ANGRY when another car bumped his.
Tengo la entrevista mañana y estoy muy nervioso.	My interview is tomorrow and I'm really NERVOUS!

Never

Never is always negative. For its position in the sentence, see WORD ORDER (2). It cannot be used together with another negative, see NEGATIVES. It is often confused with *ever*, which means *at any time*, particularly with the Present Perfect tense. (But notice: *hardly ever* = 'casi nunca'.)

Es la ciudad más bonita que haya visto jamás.	⊗It's the most beautiful city I've never seen.⊗ (This means that you haven't seen the city!)
	It's the most beautiful city I've EVER seen.
Nunca he visto una ciudad tan bonita.	I've NEVER seen such a beautiful city.

Notice the difference between:

¿Has estado alguna vez en París?	Have you EVER been to Paris?

and:

¿Nunca has estado en París?	Have you NEVER been to Paris? (expressing surprise)
Casi nunca sale (de casa).	⊗He hardly never goes out.⊗
	He hardly EVER goes out.

News

See also NOTICE.

News ('noticias') is singular and uncountable. To translate 'una noticia', we have to say *a piece of news*, *an item of news*, *some news* etc.

Acabo de oír una mala noticia.	⊗I've just heard a bad news.⊗
	I've just heard SOME bad news.

La noticia fue terrible: 300 muertos.	⊗The new was terrible: 300 people killed.⊗ The NEWS was terrible: 300 people killed.
Mira esta noticia; es muy interesante.	⊗Look at this new – it's very interesting.⊗ Look at this (PIECE OF) NEWS – it's very interesting.

Next
See also LAST.

(1) *Next* is used without *the* and without a preposition, when referring to the week/month/year etc. after this one.

Nos veremos la semana que viene.	⊗I'll see you the next week.⊗ I'll see you NEXT WEEK.
Hemos quedado para el martes que viene.	⊗We're meeting on next Tuesday.⊗ We're meeting NEXT Tuesday.

(2) It can be used with *the* when referring to *the next of a series*, either in the past or the future; and also when it means a period starting now.

Se sacó el carnet de conducir en abril, y al mes siguiente se compró un Volvo nuevo.	He passed his driving test in April, and THE NEXT month (he) bought a new Volvo.
Creo que los próximos 12 meses van a ser muy difíciles.	I think THE NEXT year will be a very hard one.

(3) Where in Spanish the proximity of a date is indicated by 'el próximo. . .', English uses only the date itself.

El partido se jugará el próximo día 5 (de diciembre).	⊗The match will be played the next 5th December.⊗ The match will be played ON 5th December.

No, not

No is a determiner, used with a noun. *Not* is used to form the negative of a verb.

Puedo ir hoy pero mañana no.	⊗I can go today but no tomorrow.⊗ I can go today but NOT tomorrow (i.e. I CAN'T GO tomorrow.)
No tenía ni idea.	⊗He had not idea (about it).⊗ He had NO idea (about it).
La radio no tiene pilas.	⊗There are not batteries in the radio.⊗ There are NO batteries in the radio. (or: There AREN'T ANY batteries in the radio.)

¿No?
See TAG QUESTIONS

Nobody
See NEGATIVES (1)

No one

No one and *none* are often confused. *No one* means *nobody* and refers to people only. It cannot be followed by *of*. *None* can refer to people or things and means *not one of*.

Ninguno de mis amigos vino a verme al hospital.	⊗No one of my friends came to visit me in hospital.⊗ NONE of my friends came to visit me in hospital.
–¿Cuántas novelas de A. Christie has leído? *–Ninguna.*	'How many Agatha Christie books have you read?' ⊗'No one.'⊗ 'NONE.'
Esperé una hora pero no vino nadie.	I waited for an hour but NO ONE/NOBODY came.

Note

A *note* most commonly is a written message you leave somebody if you can't see them personally; students can *take notes* in class when the teacher explains something; but 'nota(s)' for an exam is *mark(s)*.

Estoy muy decepcionado: he sacado muy malas notas.	⊗I'm very disappointed: I've got very bad notes.⊗ I'm very disappointed: I've got very bad MARKS.
Dejo esta nota para John: por favor, díselo cuando venga.	I'm leaving this NOTE for John: will you tell him when he comes?

Nothing

See NEGATIVES (1)

Notice

A *notice* is written information which you would find outside a building, on an office wall, on a door etc. It does not translate 'una noticia'.

¿Has oído la noticia? Ha habido un terremoto en Japón.	⊗Have you heard the notice?⊗ There's been an earthquake in Japan. Have you heard the NEWS? There's been an earthquake in Japan.
Aviso: Este despacho está abierto al público entre las 10 y las 17 horas.	NOTICE: This office is open to the public between the hours of 10 a.m. and 5 p.m.

Nowadays

Nowadays is used to described a *trend* or *custom* or a prolonged action. It is not used when speaking about an action which takes place at one specific moment.

El jefe quiere verte ahora.	⊗The boss wants to see you nowadays.⊗ The boss wants to see you NOW.

Hoy en día va menos gente al cine. — NOWADAYS fewer people go to the cinema (than before).

Numbers

There are 4 common mistakes with numbers.

(1) Not using *and* for numbers in the hundreds.

Está en la página 235. — ⊗It's on page two hundred thirty-five.⊗
It's on page two hundred AND thirty-five.

(2) Using *million* with *of*, or in the plural form after a specific number.

Cuesta 2 millones de pesetas. — ⊗It costs two millions of pesetas.⊗
It costs two MILLION pesetas.

but notice:

Hay millones de africanos muriéndose de hambre. — There are MILLIONS OF Africans starving to death.

(3) The word order in expressions like 'los 3 primeros'.

Los dos primeros ejercicios son muy difíciles. — ⊗The two first exercises are very difficult.⊗
The FIRST TWO exercises are very difficult.

(4) The translation of expressions indicating how many people are/were in a place.

Éramos 20 en la fiesta. — ⊗We were 20 people at the party.⊗
THERE WERE 20 OF US at the party.

Eran 6 en el grupo. — ⊗They were 6 in the group.⊗
THERE WERE 6 OF THEM in the group.

O

To offer

We say *to offer somebody something* or *to offer to do something (for somebody)* but we cannot say *to offer somebody to do something*.

Le ofrecieron que se quedara algunos días en casa. — ⊗They offered him to stay with them for a few days.⊗
They offered TO LET HIM STAY with them for a few days.
(or: They OFFERED HIM A BED for a few days.)

Se ofreció para ayudarles. — ⊗He offered them to help them.⊗
He OFFERED TO HELP them.

One

When we use *one* with a noun, we mean *only one, not two or three.* If we are referring simply to an indefinite singular noun, we must use the determiner *a(n).*

Vi a un hombre pasear por la calle.	⊗I saw one man walking down the street.⊗
	I saw A man walking down the street.
Solamente había un coche aparcado delante del hotel.	⊗There was only a car parked outside the hotel.⊗
	There was only ONE car parked outside the hotel.

One time

We normally say *once*, not *one time*, to refer to the number of times a thing is done. *One time* normally means *on one occasion*.

Sólo he estado en Roma una vez.	⊗I've only been to Rome one time.⊗
	I've only been to Rome ONCE.
'Llame (Una Vez) Antes de Entrar'	⊗'Knock One Time and Enter'⊗
	'Knock ONCE And Enter'
Me acuerdo de una ocasión cuando era muy joven. . . .	I remember ONE TIME when I was very young. . . .

Only See ALONE

Opened

Opened is a verb, the past form of *to open*, and is therefore only used for the action of opening. The adjective is *open*, which never changes form, whether it refers to a present or past situation.

La puerta ya estaba abierta cuando llegaron.	⊗When they arrived, the door was already opened.⊗
	When they arrived, the door was already OPEN.
La puerta fue abierta por el portero.	The door was OPENED by the caretaker.

Other(s)

(1) *Other* is followed by a plural noun, except when it is used with *the* and is specific; with a singular noun, we must use *another*.

¿Puedes darme otro libro?	⊗Can you give me other book?⊗
	Can you give me ANOTHER book?
Vi a María el otro día.	I saw Mary THE OTHER day.
Compré una silla, un armario y otras cosas.	I bought a chair, a wardrobe and OTHER things.

(2) *Others* is a pronoun, not an adjective.

Vi a Paul, a John y a otros amigos.	⊗I saw Paul, John and others friends.⊗ I saw Paul, John and OTHER friends.
A algunos les gustan las películas movidas: otros prefieren historias de amor.	Some people like action films: OTHERS prefer romantic films.

(3) *Another* and not *other* is used with a plural noun if it is accompanied by a number or *few*.

Voy a quedarme aquí 3 días más.	⊗I'm going to stay here other three days.⊗ I'm going to stay here ANOTHER three days.
Da tres pasos más adelante.	⊗Move forward other 3 paces.⊗ Move forward ANOTHER 3 paces.

Ought to

See also MODAL AUXILIARY VERBS

Ought to has virtually the same meaning as *should* when talking about obligation, probability or giving advice. Remember, it is the only modal auxiliary verb which can be followed by *to*.

Deberías echarte si te duele la cabeza.	⊗You ought lie down if you've got a headache.⊗ You OUGHT TO lie down if you've got a headache.

P

Paper

Paper in English means simply the substance we use to make books etc. or, as an abbreviation, *newspaper*. It is uncountable; 'una hoja' is *a sheet/piece of paper*. 'Un papel' in the cinema or theatre is a *role* or *part*, used with the verb *to play*.

¿Qué periódico lees?	What (NEWS)PAPER do you read?
¿Me dejas una hoja?	⊗Can you give me a paper?⊗ Can you give me a SHEET/PIECE of paper?
¿Qué papel hizo en esa película?	⊗What paper did she make in the film?⊗ What PART/ROLE did she PLAY in the film?

Particular

Particular means *specific* or *in particular*; to translate the Spanish word 'particular' meaning *not public*, we must say *private*.

Estudia francés con un profesor particular.	⊗He studies French with a particular teacher.⊗ He studies French with a PRIVATE teacher.

¿Qué titulación se exige para este trabajo, en concreto?	What PARTICULAR qualifications are required for the job?

Party
See also TO CELEBRATE

We say *to go to a party* but *to be at a party* (not *in*). People *have (or give) a party*, not *do*, *make* or *celebrate*.

Hubo mucha gente interesante en la fiesta.	⊗There were a lot of interesting people in the party.⊗
	There were a lot of interesting people AT the party.
Hicimos/Celebramos una fiesta para el cumpleaños de Mary.	⊗We made/did a party for Mary's birthday.⊗
	We HAD a party for Mary's birthday.

To pass

We say that time *passes* but that someone *spends* time doing something (except in the expression *to do something to pass the time*, which indicates that the subject is feeling bored, and does not indicate how long the action continues).

Pasé un fin de semana muy bonito en la Costa Brava.	⊗I passed a lovely weekend on the Costa Brava.⊗
	I SPENT a lovely weekend on the Costa Brava.
El tiempo pasa muy rápido.	Time PASSES very quickly.
Mientras esperaban, jugaban a cartas para pasar el tiempo.	While they were waiting, they played cards TO PASS THE TIME.

To pay (for)

(1) The verb *to pay* must be followed by *for* when you say the item or article that is bought.

¿Has pagado la cámara?	⊗Have you paid the camera?⊗
	Have you paid FOR the camera?
He pagado la cuenta.	⊗I've paid for the bill.⊗
	I've PAID the bill.
	(You don't buy the bill.)

(2) It is not followed by *to* when used with people.

La empresa paga a sus empleados a finales de mes.	⊗The company pays to its employees at the end of the month.⊗
	The company PAYS its employees at the end of the month.

(3) You cannot *pay for somebody something*: we say *to buy somebody something* (e.g. a drink or a meal).

Te pago una copa/Te invito a una copa.	⊗I'll pay you a drink/I'll pay a drink for you.⊗
	I'll BUY YOU a drink.

People

People takes a plural verb in English.

La gente es muy simpática.	⊗The people is very friendly.⊗ The people ARE very friendly.
¿Cuántas personas resultaron heridas en el accidente?	⊗How many people was hurt in the accident?⊗ How many people WERE hurt in the accident?

Persons

We normally use the plural form of *person* only in very formal language; it is much more common to use *people*.

Había unas 20 personas en la cola.	⊗There were about 20 persons in the queue. (unusual)⊗ There were about 20 PEOPLE in the queue.
'Peso máximo: 4 personas.' (en un ascensor.)	'Weight limit: 4 PERSONS.' (Sign in a lift.)

Photo(graph)

We say *to take*, not *make*, a photo(graph).

¿Hiciste muchas fotos durante las vacaciones?	⊗Did you make many photos on your holidays?⊗ Did you TAKE many photos on your holidays?

Pilot

A *pilot* flies a plane: for a car, we say *(racing) driver*.

Nelson Piquet es un gran piloto.	⊗Nelson Piquet is a great pilot.⊗ Nelson Piquet is a great (RACING) DRIVER.

Play

'Jugar' is *to play* but 'un juego' is *a game* and 'un juguete' is *a toy*. The noun *a play* refers to the theatre.

El frontón es un juego tradicional del País Vasco.	⊗Frontón is a traditional play in the Basque Country.⊗ Frontón is a traditional GAME in the Basque Country.
El niño estaba contento con sus juguetes.	The baby was PLAYING happily with his TOYS.
Para mí, 'Macbeth' es la mejor obra de Shakespeare.	I think 'Macbeth' is Shakespeare's best PLAY.

Plenty (of)

Plenty (of) expresses quantity and is used with uncountable or plural nouns. It cannot be used as an adjective to describe e.g. a room or a bus etc. which contain a large number of people: for this, we use *full* or *crowded*.

La playa estaba llena.	⊗The beach was plenty of people.⊗
	The beach was FULL of people. (or: The beach was CROWDED.)
El cuarto estaba tan lleno que apenas podía moverme.	⊗The room was so plenty that I could hardly move.⊗
	The room was so FULL/CROWDED that I could hardly move.
Tenemos pan y queso de sobra pero necesitamos más mantequilla.	We have PLENTY OF bread and cheese but we need more butter.

Police

The police refers to the body of police and is followed by a plural verb; the individual is *a policeman/policewoman*, which of course takes a singular verb.

La policía es muy dura aquí.	⊗The police is very strict here.⊗
	The police ARE very strict here.
Un policía me pidió el carnet de conducir.	⊗A police asked to see my driving licence.⊗
	A POLICEMAN asked to see my driving licence.

Possible

It is very uncommon in English to use *it is possible. . .* with a future tense to express a possible action: for this, we normally use *might* or *may*, followed by an infinitive without *to*.

Es posible que me vaya fuera el próximo fin de semana.	⊗It is possible that I will go away next weekend.⊗ (very uncommon)
	I MIGHT/MAY GO away next weekend.

To prefer

We *prefer* someone/something *to* someone/something else.

Prefiero el fútbol al tenis.	⊗I prefer football than tennis.⊗
	I prefer football TO tennis.
Prefiere comer fuera a preparar la comida en casa.	⊗He prefers eating out than making meals at home.⊗
	He prefers eating out TO making meals at home.

To prepare

We can say *to prepare a meal/a class* (speaking about a teacher)/*a room* (for a visitor) etc. but not *to prepare a party* (we *get ready for* or *prepare things for a party*), or *to prepare an exam* (we say *to prepare for* or, more commonly, *to study for* an exam).

Durante toda la tarde preparamos la fiesta.	⊗We prepared the party all afternoon.⊗ We GOT (THINGS) READY FOR the party all afternoon.
No puedo salir este fin de semana, tengo que preparar un examen.	⊗I can't go out this weekend, I have to prepare an exam.⊗ I can't go out this weekend, I have to STUDY FOR an exam.
Los anfitriones prepararon una cena magnífica.	The hosts PREPARED a magnificent dinner.

Presently

Presently (or *shortly*) means *soon, in a few moments*, not *now* or *at the moment*.

Actualmente vivimos en Viena.	⊗Presently, we are living in Vienna.⊗ AT THE MOMENT (or AT PRESENT) we are living in Vienna.
La cena estará lista dentro de poco.	Dinner will be ready PRESENTLY/SHORTLY/SOON.

Present perfect simple See also SINCE

The *Present Perfect* tense is most commonly confused with two other tenses.

(1) The *Present Perfect*, not the Present tense, is used for an action which started in the past and continues into the present.

Hace 3 años que vivo en Barcelona.	⊗I live/am living in Barcelona for 3 years.⊗ I HAVE LIVED/HAVE BEEN LIVING in Barcelona for 3 years.

(2) The *Present Perfect* is not used when we talk about a finished action which took place at a specific moment. In this case, we use the simple past.

However, if the action took place at an indeterminate moment in the past and is in some way related to the present, the Present Perfect is used.

Estuve en Tailandia en 1985.	⊗I have been in Thailand in 1985.⊗ I WAS in Thailand in 1985. (Specific time.)
He estado en Tailandia varias veces.	⊗I was in Thailand several times.⊗ I HAVE BEEN TO/IN Thailand several times. (Indeterminate time.)

(3) We also use the Present Perfect if the period of time we are talking about is still continuing.

Compare:

Te he llamado esta mañana pero no estabas.	⊗I have phoned you this morning, but you weren't in.⊗ I PHONED you this morning, but you weren't in. (it's now afternoon/evening.)

with:

He trabajado mucho esta mañana.	⊗I worked a lot this morning.⊗ I HAVE WORKED a lot this morning. (it's still morning.)

Present perfect continuous

In many cases, the *Present Perfect Continuous* can be used in the same way as the Present Perfect Simple, although the Continuous form, logically, puts some emphasis on the continuity of the action. However, the Continuous form is not used in the following circumstances.

(1) When we express the idea of completion (e.g. an action which has just been finished).

He leído ese libro.	⊗I have been reading that book.⊗ I HAVE READ that book. (I've finished it.)

(2) When we say the number of times an action has happened, or the number of things that have been done.

Compare:

Esta mañana he fumado 10 cigarrillos.	⊗I have been smoking ten cigarettes this morning.⊗ I HAVE SMOKED ten cigarettes this morning.

With:

He estado fumando toda la mañana.	I'VE BEEN SMOKING all morning.

To pretend

To pretend means *to give the false appearance of doing or being something* (= 'disimular'/'fingir'). It does not translate 'pretender hacer': for this, we use *to try* or *to attempt*.

¿Que pretendes conseguir?	⊗What are you pretending to achieve?⊗ What are you TRYING to achieve?
El niño fingió estar enfermo porque no tenía ganas de ir al colegio.	The little boy PRETENDED he was ill because he didn't want to go to school.

To prove

To prove means *to demonstrate with evidence*, e.g. scientifically or statistically. But we say *to try* a new kind of food or drink (e.g.) and *to try on* clothes.

¿Quieres probar esta sopa?	⊗Would you like to prove this soup?⊗ Would you like to TRY this soup?
Se probó el vestido.	⊗She proved the dress.⊗ She TRIED the dress ON.
La policía demostró que el sospechoso había mentido.	The police PROVED that the suspect had lied.

Q

Question

We say *to ask a question*, not *to make a question*.

Me hizo muchas preguntas.	⊗She made me a lot of questions.⊗ She ASKED me a lot of questions.

Quite

Quite can be used with two meanings.

(1) *Completely*, when used with a strong or extreme adjective, e.g. impossible/brilliant/superb/exhausted etc.

La orquesta es magnífica.	The orchestra is QUITE brilliant.

(2) Perhaps more commonly, meaning *moderately*.

El libro es bastante bueno pero no es el mejor de los que ha escrito.	The book is QUITE good, but not his best.

(3) *Rather* has a similar meaning to (2) but it is often used with a stronger meaning than *quite*, both positively and negatively.

Es un poco bajo para jugar al baloncesto.	⊗He's quite small to play basketball.⊗ He's RATHER small to play basketball.
Hay demasiada gente aquí: ¿Por qué no salimos fuera?	It's RATHER crowded in here – let's go outside. (*quite* is possible here, but *rather* is better).
Me gusta este libro.	This book is RATHER good.

(4) With comparatives, only *rather* can be used.

Su nueva película es bastante mejor que las que hizo hace diez años.	⊗His new film is quite better than the ones he made ten years ago.⊗ His new film is RATHER better than the ones he made ten years ago.

R

To raise See TO RISE

Rare

Rare means *not common*, something which does not happen often. 'Una persona rara' is a *strange* or *funny* person.

Es una persona muy rara.	⊗He's a very rare person.⊗ He's a very STRANGE person.
El águila imperial es poco frecuente.	The Imperial Eagle is RARE.
Mi primo nos visitó la semana pasada por primera vez en mucho tiempo.	We had a RARE visit from my cousin last week.

Rather, I'd

I would (I'd) rather. . . means *I would prefer to. . .* but is not followed by *to*:

–¿Te apetece salir esta noche?–	"Would you like to come out tonight?"
–No gracias, prefiero quedarme en casa.	⊗"No thanks, I'd rather to stay at home."⊗ "No, thanks, I'd rather STAY (or: I'd prefer TO STAY) at home."

Receipt See also TICKET

You get a *receipt* in a shop when you buy something; if you want to change this article later, you have to show this *receipt*.
When you are ill, the doctor gives you a *prescription* for medicine.
A *recipe* tells you how to cook a meal/dish.
You pay the *bill* in a hotel or restaurant, or every month for gas/electricity/water.

El médico me dió una receta para comprar pastillas.	⊗The doctor gave me a receipt for some tablets.⊗ The doctor gave me a PRESCRIPTION for some tablets.
¡El pastel estaba buenísimo! ¿Me das la receta?	That cake was delicious! ⊗Can you give me the receipt?⊗ That cake was delicious! Can you give me the RECIPE?
¡No te olvides de pagar el recibo del gas!	⊗Don't forget to pay the gas receipt!⊗ Don't forget to pay the gas BILL!
He perdido el recibo de la radio que compré la semana pasada.	I've lost the RECEIPT for the radio I bought last week.

Reflexive pronouns

A common mistake is to use the ordinary object pronoun instead of the reflexive pronoun after a reflexive verb.

Me corté cuando me afeitaba. ⊗I cut me while I was shaving.⊗

I cut MYSELF while I was shaving.

Todos debemos preguntarnos cómo podemos ayudar a los que pasan hambre. ⊗We must all ask us how we can help the starving.⊗

We must all ask OURSELVES how we can help the starving.

Se miró en el espejo. ⊗He looked at him in the mirror.⊗

He looked at HIMSELF in the mirror.

To refuse

See TO DENY

To relax

In English, *relax* is only used as a verb, not as a noun. The verb is not reflexive.

Necesito relajarme. ⊗I need a relax./I need to relax me.⊗

I need TO relax.

Relájate, tómatelo con calma. RELAX, take it easy.

To remark

To remark is a verb of saying, not of seeing. It is most commonly used after direct speech in written English, when it is an alternative for *said*.

No vi nada extraño en la casa. ⊗I didn't remark anything strange about the house.⊗

I didn't NOTICE anything strange about the house.

-Qué día más bonito- dijo. "It's a lovely day," he REMARKED.

To remember

(1) You *remember* a person/a place/a past action/to do something.

No recuerdo nada de la película. ⊗I can't remind anything about the film.⊗

I can't REMEMBER anything about the film.

Tengo que acordarme de llamar a John. ⊗I must remind to ring John.⊗

I must REMEMBER to ring John.

Recuerdos a tus padres. ⊗Remind me to your parents.⊗

REMEMBER me to your parents.

(2) You *remind* someone to do something, or something *reminds* you of something; *to remind* is always followed by a noun or pronoun.

Recuérdame que eche esa carta al correo. ⊗Remember me to post that letter.⊗

REMIND me to post that letter.

Esa foto me recuerda a un viejo amigo mío.	⊗That photo remembers me of an old friend of mine.⊗
	That photo REMINDS me of an old friend of mine.

(3) You *remember doing something* for a past action; you *remember to do something* for an action which is future at the time of speaking.

¿Te acuerdas cuando tuvimos que esperar 10 horas en el aeropuerto?	⊗Do you remember to wait 10 hours at the airport?⊗
	Do you remember WAITING 10 hours (or: WHEN WE WAITED 10 hours) at the airport?
Acuérdate de apagarlo todo antes de marchar.	⊗Remember switching everything off before you leave.⊗
	Remember TO SWITCH everything off before you leave.

To remind See TO REMEMBER

To rent

You *rent* a flat or house if you are paying money to live there; if the property is yours, and another person pays you money to live there, you *let* it (*out*).

Mientras estaba en EE.UU. alquiló su piso.	⊗He rented his flat out while he was in the United States.⊗
	He LET his flat out while he was in the United States.
Busca un piso de alquiler.	He's looking for a flat to RENT.

Reported questions

There are two main problems for students with *reported (indirect) questions.*

(1) The auxiliary verbs *do* or *did*, used in direct questions, must be removed.

–¿Dónde vives?– me preguntó.	'Where do you live?' he asked.
Me preguntó dónde vivía.	⊗He asked me where do/did I live.⊗
	He asked me where I LIVE/LIVED.
–¿Qué hiciste el fin de semana pasado?–	"What did you do last weekend?"
Le preguntó qué había hecho el fin de semana pasado/anterior.	⊗She asked him what did he do last weekend.⊗
	She asked him what HE DID last weekend. (or: what HE HAD DONE THE PREVIOUS weekend).

(2) The verb *to be* reverts to its normal position, i.e. after the subject.

–¿Dónde está la estación?– preguntó.	"Where is the station?" he asked.
Preguntó dónde estaba la estación.	⊗He asked where was the station.⊗
	He asked where the station WAS.

–¿Dónde viven ahora?–	"Where are they living now?"
Quería saber dónde vivían entonces.	⊗She wanted to know where were they living then.⊗
	She wanted to know where THEY WERE living then.

To rest

To rest means *to relax*, *to take it easy*, *not to work* etc. It does not mean *to stay*.

No salgo esta noche; me quedo en casa.	⊗I'm not going out tonight: I'm going to rest at home.⊗
	I'm not going out tonight: I'm going to STAY at home.
El médico me ha dicho que debo descansar en casa.	The doctor has told me I must REST at home.

Reunion

In English, *reunion* has a very specific meaning; a group of people meeting, once a year for example, to celebrate some special event from the past, e.g. an old school reunion, the reunion of War Veterans, etc. To translate 'una reunión', we say *meeting*.

Tengo una reunión (de negocios) a las 9.	⊗I have a business reunion at 9.00.⊗
	I have a business MEETING at 9.00.
La reunión anual de los Veteranos de Guerra tendrá lugar en abril.	The Annual War Veterans REUNION will take place in April.

To rise

To rise (*rose*, *risen*) is an intransitive verb, i.e. it cannot have an object. *To raise* (regular verb) is transitive – it must have an object.

En verano el sol sale a las 5.	⊗In summer, the sun raises at 5 a.m.⊗
	In summer, the sun RISES at 5 a.m.
Si sabes la respuesta, levanta la mano.	⊗If you know the answer, rise your hand.⊗
	If you know the answer, RAISE your hand.

NB: *Rise* can be used in the sense of *to get up* ('levantarse') but this is not common in modern English.

To rob

You can *rob* a person or place but not a thing; when we mention the article taken, we must use *to steal* – see TO STEAL.

Le robaron su coche nuevo.	⊗His new car was robbed.⊗
	His new car was STOLEN.

Me robaron en Londres la semana pasada.	⊗I was stolen in London last week.⊗
	I was ROBBED in London last week.
Cinco hombres robaron el banco.	Five men ROBBED the bank.
Robaron $5000.	⊗They robbed $5000.⊗
	They STOLE $5000.

S

Same

(1) *Same* is always used with *the*. Before a following noun or pronoun, we use *as*, not *than* or *that* (although *that* can be used before a clause).

A él le gusta la misma música que a mí.	⊗He likes the same music that/than me.⊗
	He likes the same music AS me.
Para él, era el mismo problema de siempre.	It was the same problem (THAT) he had always had.

(2) The translation of 'da igual'/'(me) da lo mismo' is *it doesn't matter*, (although the expression *it's all the same to me* does exist).

–¿Qué día te va mejor, el sábado o el domingo?	"Which day is better for you – Saturday or Sunday?"
–(Me) da igual.	⊗"It's/Is the same."⊗
	"IT DOESN'T MATTER." (or: "IT'S ALL THE SAME TO ME".)

(3) To translate 'mismo' when emphasizing that a specific person, and nobody else, does an action, we use the reflexive pronoun *myself/himself/themselves* etc., not *the same*.

Los mismos Reyes le recibieron en la puerta.	⊗The same King and Queen met him at the door.⊗
	The King and Queen THEMSELVES met him at the door.

To say See also TO TELL

To say is often confused with *to tell*.

(1) *To say* is normally used without a personal object (*me*, *him*, *the man* etc.). If the personal object is present, *to* must be used before it.

Me dijo que era de Londres.	⊗She said me (that) she was from London.⊗
	She TOLD me (that) she was from London.
–Buenos días– les dijo a todos.	⊗"Good morning," she said everybody.⊗
	"Good morning," she said TO everybody.

(2) It is not used in certain expressions where *to tell* must be used – *to tell a lie/ a story/ the truth/ the time* are the most common.

Siempre deberías decir la verdad.	⊗You should always say the truth.⊗ You should always TELL the truth.
–Papá, ¡cuéntanos un cuento!	⊗"Say us a story, dad!"⊗ "TELL us a story, dad!"

(3) It cannot be used in indirect questions or commands.

Me preguntó si quería ir al teatro.	⊗She said me if I wanted to go to the theatre.⊗ She ASKED me if I wanted to go to the theatre.
Les dije que se diesen prisa.	⊗I said them to hurry up.⊗ I TOLD them to hurry up.

To seem

(1) 'Parecer' can be translated by the verb *to seem*, but normally only in a general sense – if there is a visual idea, we prefer to use *to look*; if we are talking about our impression of a person or place after hearing information about them, we prefer to use *to sound*.

–¡Qué foto más buena! Parece un pueblo muy bonito.	⊗What a great photo! It seems a very nice village.⊗ (not incorrect but uncommon). What a great photo! It LOOKS a very nice village.
–Por lo visto has pasado unas vacaciones estupendas.	⊗"Your holiday seems great."⊗ "Your holiday SOUNDS great."
Por lo que dices tu jefe es simpático (yo no lo conozco).	⊗Your boss seems a nice man.⊗ Your boss SOUNDS a nice man.
Tu jefe parece simpático. (Acabo de conocerlo y es mi primera impresión.)	Your boss SEEMS a nice man.

(2) All 3 verbs above are used with adjectives, not adverbs. (see ADJECTIVES (4)).

La casa es/parece bonita.	⊗The house looks nicely.⊗ The house looks NICE.
Tu nuevo trabajo parece bueno.	⊗Your new job sounds well.⊗ Your new job sounds GOOD.

(3) Before a noun with no adjective, we use *to seem to be* or *to look like*.

Parece que es el jefe.	⊗He seems the manager.⊗ He SEEMS TO BE the manager. (or: He LOOKS LIKE the manager.)

Sensible

Sensible translates the Spanish 'sensato'; to translate 'sensible', we say *sensitive* in English.

No le critiques, es muy sensible.

⊗Don't criticise him – he's very sensible.⊗

Don't criticise him – he's very SENSITIVE.

Esa chica es muy sensata, tiene mucho sentido común.

⊗She's a very sensitive girl – she has a lot of common sense.⊗

She's a very SENSIBLE girl – she has a lot of common sense.

Sensitive See SENSIBLE

Shopping See TO BUY

Should See MODAL AUXILIARY VERBS

Similar

The preposition used after *similar* is *to*, not *than*.

Tu bolso es muy parecido al mío.

⊗Your bag is very similar than mine.⊗

Your bag is very similar TO mine.

El portugués escrito es bastante parecido al español.

⊗Written Portuguese is quite similar than Spanish.⊗

Written Portuguese is quite similar TO Spanish.

Simple past See PRESENT PERFECT

Since

Since is very often confused with (1)*for* and (2)*from*.

(1) With the Present Perfect or Past Perfect tense, *for* indicates how long an action or situation has lasted; *since* indicates the point of time when the action started. Notice that we do not use the Present tense. (see also PRESENT PERFECT).

Hace 3 años que aprende inglés. (Aprende inglés desde 1984/julio/las pasadas Navidades etc.)

⊗She has been learning English since 3 years (ago).⊗

She has been learning English FOR 3 years. (or: SINCE 1984/July/last Christmas, etc.)

Hacía 45 minutos que le esperaba cuando por fin llegó.

⊗I'd been waiting since 45 minutes when he finally arrived.⊗

I'd been waiting FOR 45 minutes when he finally arrived (or: I'd been waiting SINCE 8.00 etc.)

Llevo esperando desde las 4 (y aún estoy esperando).

⊗I am waiting since 4.00.⊗

I HAVE BEEN WAITING SINCE 4.00. (and I'm still·waiting)

(2) If the situation has now finished, or is in the future, we use *from* instead of *since*. Very often, *from* is used with *till/until* when we indicate both when the action started/will start and finished/will finish.

Estaré en el despacho a partir de las 3 si quieres llamarme.

⊗I'll be at the office since 3.00 if you want to ring me.⊗

I'll be at the office FROM 3.00 if you want to ring me.

Me quedé allí desde el viernes hasta el lunes.

⊗I stayed there since Friday to/till/until Monday.⊗

I stayed there FROM Friday to/till/until Monday.

So (1)

So is used to qualify an adjective or adverb on their own; *such (a)* must be used before a noun or before an adjective and noun together.

¡Es una ciudad tan tranquila!

⊗It is a so quiet town.⊗

It is SUCH A quiet town.

No me gusta la gente así.

⊗I don't like so people.⊗

I don't like SUCH people.

¡París es tan bonito!

Paris is so beautiful!

¡Toca el piano tan bien!

He plays the piano so beautifully!

So (2)

When agreeing with an affirmative statement which has gone before, we often use *so* (as the first word) with an auxiliary verb (or *to be*) before the subject. (See TAG QUESTIONS for rules on which auxiliary verb to use).

–Me gusta la carne.
–A mí también.

"I like meat."
⊗"So like I."/⊗
⊗"So I like."/"So I do."⊗
"SO DO I."

–El verano pasado fui a Bulgaria.
–¿Ah sí? Yo también.

"I went to Bulgaria last summer."
⊗"So went I."/"So I went."/⊗
⊗"So I did."⊗
"(Did you?) SO DID I."

Soap

Soap = 'jabón', *soup* = 'sopa'. Be careful in a restaurant!

A menudo como sopa al mediodía.

⊗I often have soap for lunch.⊗

I often have SOUP for lunch.

Nos lavamos con jabón.

⊗You use soup to wash yourself.⊗

You use SOAP to wash yourself.

So many

See SO MUCH

So much

(1) *So much/many* ('tanto(s)') are used in a very similar way to *much/many* (see MUCH), but they are very normal in affirmative sentences.

Hay tanto tráfico en el centro de la ciudad.	There is SO MUCH traffic in the city centre.

(2) They cannot be used before an adjective without a noun: for this, we use *so*.

¡Es tan caro comprar un coche nuevo!	⊗Buying a new car is so much expensive!⊗ Buying a new car is SO expensive!

Some See also ANY

The simple "rule" that *some* is affirmative and *any* negative or interrogative is not always true. *Some* can be used in questions when we are expecting a positive answer, or when we are thinking of a particular quantity or amount of something.

Mi abuela me dejó dinero.	My grandmother left me SOME money.
No llevo dinero encima.	I haven't got ANY money with me.
¿Puedes dejarme (un poco de) dinero para el autobús?	⊗Can you lend me any money for the bus?⊗ Can you lend me SOME money for the bus? (you are confident that the answer will be "yes", and you are thinking of a particular sum of money, e.g. 50p. The question 'Can you lend me ANY money?' means that you are not sure of the answer and have no fixed sum in mind.)
¿Tienen plátanos?	⊗Have you got some bananas?⊗ Have you got ANY bananas? (In a shop – you don't know if they have bananas or not.)
¿Te apetece un té?	⊗Would you like any tea?⊗ Would you like SOME tea? (You are thinking of a cup of tea.)
¿Tenemos té (en casa)?	Have we got ANY tea in the house? (You don't know if you have or not.)
¿Podrás traer discos a la fiesta?	Can you bring ANY records to the party? (You don't know if he has records or not.)
Trae algunos discos tuyos a la fiesta. ¿Quieres?	Can you bring SOME (of your) records to the party? (You know that he has records and can probably bring some to the party.)

To sound

(1) The translation of 'me suena' is *it/that sounds familiar* or *I've heard of it/him/her* etc..

Me suena su nombre.	⊗His name sounds me.⊗ His name SOUNDS FAMILIAR (to me). (or: I'VE HEARD HIS/THAT NAME.)

Specially

Specially means *for a specific reason* (= 'expresamente').
Especially means *in particular* or *above all* (= 'sobre todo').

Llueve mucho en invierno, sobre todo en el norte.	⊗It rains heavily in winter, specially in the north.⊗ It rains heavily in winter, ESPECIALLY in the north.
Ha venido expresamente a verte.	⊗He has come especially to see you.⊗ He has come SPECIALLY to see you.

To spend

The 2 things we most commonly spend are time and money. For time, see TO PASS. For money, we say *to spend money ON something/someone*, not *in*.

Se han gastado mucho dinero en la nueva casa.	⊗They've spent a lot of money in their new house.⊗ They've spent a lot of money ON their new house.

(In) spite of

In spite of (or *despite*) is followed by a gerund or by a phrase (containing a noun or pronoun but no verb), but not by a clause (containing a full subject and verb); with a clause, we use *although* (or *though*).

A pesar de la lluvia, fueron a pasear.	⊗Despite/in spite (of) it was raining, they went out for a walk.⊗ IN SPITE OF THE RAIN (or: DESPITE THE RAIN), they went out for a walk.
Aunque llovía, fueron a pasear.	ALTHOUGH IT WAS RAINING, they went out for a walk.
A pesar de ser rico/Aunque era rico, no era muy generoso.	⊗In spite of he was rich, he wasn't very generous.⊗ IN SPITE OF BEING rich, he wasn't very generous. (or: ALTHOUGH he was rich, he wasn't very generous.)

Station

We say a bus/train *station*, but summer and winter are *seasons* of the year, and a place where you go to ski is a skiing *resort*.

Mi padre me recogió en la estación.	My father picked me up from the STATION.
La primavera es la estación que más me gusta.	⊗Spring is my favourite station.⊗ Spring is my favourite SEASON.

Vamos a esquiar a una de las estaciones de los Alpes.	⊗We're going skiing in one of the stations in the Alps.⊗
	We're going skiing in one of the RESORTS in the Alps.

To steal

(1) A person, house or bank cannot be *stolen* – see TO ROB.

Le robaron en la calle.	⊗He was stolen in the street.⊗
	He was ROBBED in the street.

(2) You *steal* something *from* a person.

Le robaron el coche.	⊗They stole him the car.⊗
	They STOLE HIS CAR.
Robó un millón de dólares a su empresa	⊗He stole $1m to his company.⊗
	He stole $1m FROM his company.

Still

(1) For confusion between *still*, *yet* and *already*, see ALREADY.

Aún no he acabado de pintar mi dormitorio.	I STILL haven't finished painting my bedroom.
	(This suggests that it has taken longer than you expected; you have taken a long time to do it.)
Compare:	I haven't finished painting my bedroom YET.
	(This simply gives us information.)

(2) The idea that *still* is used normally in affirmative sentences, and placed in mid-sentence, while *yet* is used mostly in negative or interrogative sentences and is placed at the end of the sentence, can often help the student to avoid errors. But, *still* is used very commonly in both negative and interrogative sentences, often with the idea of surprise. Remember that *still* emphasizes continuity.

¿Todavía llevas esa chaqueta vieja?	⊗Are you wearing that old jacket yet?⊗
	Are you STILL wearing that old jacket?
	(It causes surprise that the other person CONTINUES to wear it.)

Compare:

¿Todavía tienes ese VW Golf?	Have you STILL got that VW Golf? (emphasizes continuity.)

With:

¿Te has comprado ya ese VW Golf?	Have you bought that VW Golf YET? (Asking a simple question.)

To stop

To stop doing something means *to discontinue an activity* ('dejar de hacer'); *to stop to do something* means *to stop for a reason/for the purpose of doing something* ('parar con el propósito de hacer algo').

Dejó de fumar hace 6 meses.	⊗He stopped to smoke 6 months ago.⊗ He stopped SMOKING 6 months ago.
Llegaron (en coche) a Leeds, donde pararon para comer.	They drove as far as Leeds and stopped TO HAVE LUNCH.

Strange, stranger

See also FOREIGN, FOREIGNER

Somebody who behaves illogically, or in a way we consider abnormal, is said to be *strange*; a *stranger* is somebody we don't know, or who is unfamiliar with a place; somebody from a different country is a *foreigner*.

Es un tipo extraño: un día me saluda, al día siguiente, no me hace ni caso.	He's very STRANGE: one day he says hello, the next, he completely ignores me.
–¿Me puede indicar donde está la estación? No soy de aquí.	⊗"Can you tell me the way to the station, please? I'm strange here."⊗ ". . . I'm A STRANGER here."
Claro que no te entiende: es extranjero.	⊗Of course he doesn't understand you – he's a stranger/a strange.⊗ Of course he doesn't understand you – he's a FOREIGNER (or: he's FOREIGN).

Success

Success means 'éxito' and comes from the verb *to succeed*; to translate 'un suceso', we use *event* or *incident*.

Su última película fue un gran éxito.	His last film was a big SUCCESS.
Acaban de llegar noticias sobre el suceso.	⊗News about the success has just arrived.⊗ News about the EVENT has just arrived.

To suggest

To suggest is one of a number of common verbs (e.g. to say, to explain) which cannot take a personal object (me/him/them etc.). We can *suggest something* or *suggest that somebody does something* but we cannot say *suggest somebody something* or *suggest to do something*.

¿Puedes sugerirme alguna solución?	⊗Can you suggest me a solution?⊗ Can you SUGGEST a solution?
¿Por qué no te echas en la cama si estás cansado?	⊗I suggest you to lie down if you're feeling tired.⊗ I SUGGEST THAT YOU lie down if you're feeling tired. (or WHY DON'T YOU lie down. . .)

To support

You can *support* your family, a football team, a (political) cause; but to translate e.g. 'soportar una situación desagradable', we use *to bear/to stand/to put up with* etc.

No soporto a mis vecinos, siempre tienen la música altísima hasta muy tarde.	⊗I can't support my neighbours: they're always playing loud music late at night.⊗
	I can't STAND my neighbours: they're always playing loud music late at night.
Trabajaba mucho para mantener a su esposa y a sus 4 hijos.	He worked hard to SUPPORT his wife and 4 children.
Apoyo el 'Movimiento para la Paz' en ese país.	I SUPPORT the Peace Movement in that country.

Sure

Sure means a person is convinced about something, or that something is (almost) definite. In the sense of *security*, we use *safe*.

Hoy en día la gente no se siente segura en la calle.	⊗People don't feel sure in the street these days.⊗
	People don't feel SAFE in the street these days.
Ese edificio no parece muy seguro.	⊗That building doesn't look sure.⊗
	That building doesn't look SAFE.
Estoy seguro de que tendrá mucho éxito.	I'M SURE it will be a big success.
Seguro que julio será muy caluroso.	IT'S SURE to be hot in July.

Sympathetic

Sympathetic means *to show sympathy to someone*, e.g. when they are very upset about something. The normal translation of 'simpático' is *nice*, *friendly*, *pleasant* etc.

Era gente muy simpática.	⊗They were very sympathetic people.⊗
	They were very NICE/FRIENDLY people.
Mis amigos me ayudaron mucho/me dieron moral cuando murió mi padre.	My friends were very SYMPATHETIC when my father died.

T

Tag questions

In English, the way we express a *tag question* ('¿no?'/'¿verdad?') is rather complicated: it is not correct simply to use *no*?, and *isn't it*? is only used after a sentence containing *it is* (see examples (3) below). There are 6 basic rules.

(1) Normally, if the statement is affirmative, the tag question is in the negative form, and vice-versa, when we expect the listener to agree with us.

Es francesa, ¿verdad?	⊗She is French, is she?⊗ She is French, ISN'T SHE?
No vive en Londres, ¿verdad?	⊗He doesn't live in London, doesn't he?⊗ He doesn't live in London, DOES HE?

(2) If the main clause has an auxiliary verb, the tag question uses the same auxiliary verb.

Llegarán mañana, ¿no?	⊗They will arrive tomorrow, no?⊗ They will arrive tomorrow, WON'T THEY?
Te encantaría ser rico, ¿verdad?	⊗You would love to be rich, isn't it?⊗ You would love to be rich, WOULDN'T YOU?

Other examples:

No sabe nadar, ¿verdad?	He can't swim, CAN HE?
Debería descansar más, ¿verdad?	She should rest more, SHOULDN'T SHE?
Ha comprado esa casa, ¿no?	He has bought that house, HASN'T HE?

(3) If the main verb is *to be* or *to have* (= *to possess*), the tag question is also formed with *to be* or *to have*, accordingly.

Hace calor hoy, ¿verdad?	It's hot today, ISN'T IT?
Tiene un coche nuevo, ¿no?	He has (got) a new car, HASN'T HE?

(4) If there is no auxiliary verb (or *to be* or *to have*) in the main clause, we use *do/don't* for the present tense, and *did/didn't* for the past tense.

Te gusta el chocolate, ¿verdad?	You like chocolate, DON'T YOU?
Visteis la película la semana pasada, ¿no?	You saw the film last week, DIDN'T YOU?

(5) In all tag question forms, the subject and verb are inverted.

El partido no comienza hasta las 5, ¿verdad?	The match doesn't start till 5.00, DOES IT?

(6) Tag questions are not used after a real question (when we simply don't know what answer to expect).

¿Sabes ir a Edimburgo?	⊗Do you know the way to Edinburgh, do you?⊗ DO YOU KNOW the way to Edinburgh?

To take(1)

We use *to take* to express the time needed to do something, but to express the length of a film/programme/class etc., we use *to last*.

¿Cuánto dura la película?	⊗How long does the film take?⊗ How long does the film LAST?
¿Cuánto tardas en llegar al trabajo?	How long do you TAKE to get to work?

To take(2) See TO BRING

Tall

Tall is used for people and buildings, *high* for mountains, etc. (in the sense of height above sea level). If we talk about *the highest building* in a city, for example, we mean that it is built high up, e.g. on a hill.

Chicago tiene el edificio más alto del mundo.	⊗Chicago has the highest building in the world.⊗ Chicago has the TALLEST building in the world.
La Paz es la capital de mayor altitud del mundo.	La Paz is the HIGHEST capital in the world.

Team

When we talk about a specific sports team, we normally use a plural verb and no article.

El Everton es el mejor equipo de Inglaterra.	⊗The Everton is the best team in England.⊗ EVERTON ARE the best team in England.
El Barça está jugando muy bien últimamente.	⊗The Barça has been playing well recently.⊗ BARÇA HAVE been playing well recently.

To tear See TO BREAK

Television

We say *to watch something on T.V.*, not *in T.V.*.

Anoche hicieron un programa muy interesante en la tele.	⊗There was a very interesting programme in T.V. last night.⊗ There was a very interesting programme ON T.V. last night.

To tell See also TO SAY

(1) *To tell* must normally be followed by a personal direct object (but see (3) below for exceptions) and is not used with the preposition *to*.

(Me) dijo que tenía un nuevo trabajo.	⊗He told that he had a new job⊗ He TOLD ME that he had a new job. (or: He SAID that he had a new job.)
Les dijo a sus padres dónde iba.	⊗She told to her parents where she was going.⊗ She TOLD HER PARENTS where she was going.

(2) It can only be used when there is information conveyed (see also TO EXPLAIN).

-Buenos días- dijo.	⊗"Good morning," he told me.⊗ "Good morning," he SAID (TO ME).

(3) *To tell* is used instead of *to say* in certain expressions (see TO SAY (2)).

Nunca miento.	I never TELL lies.

(4) It is used with an object and infinitive in indirect commands.

Les dije que me esperasen.	⊗I told that they waited for me.⊗ I TOLD THEM TO WAIT for me.

Than

Than is used only after comparative adjectives or adverbs, or *more*. It is not used in other expressions which compare things (see also SAME and SIMILAR).

No es tan alto como yo.	⊗He's not as tall than me.⊗ He's not as tall AS me.
Es el mismo de siempre.	⊗He's just the same than ever.⊗ He's just the same AS ever.
Costó más de lo que esperaba.	It cost more THAN I expected.

That

(1) *That* can be used as a relative pronoun instead of *who(m)* (for people) and *which* (for things), but only in defining clauses, which identify the person or thing we are talking about.

Ahí está el hombre a quien le tocó la quiniela la semana pasada.	There's the man THAT/WHO won the pools last week. (This tells us which man.)
Aquella es la casa que acaban de comprar.	That's the house THAT/WHICH they have just bought. (This tells us which house.)

(2) In non-defining clauses, which simply give us more information about the person or thing we are talking about, we must use *who(m)* or *which*.

Burkina Faso, que es uno de los paises más pobres del mundo, se llamaba antes Alto Volta.	⊗Burkina Faso, that is one of the poorest countries in the world, was formerly known as Upper Volta.⊗ Burkina Faso, WHICH is one of the poorest countries in the world, was formerly known as Upper Volta. (The which clause simply gives more information about the country.)

Cary Grant, que era uno de los más conocidos actores del mundo, murió hace poco.	⊗Cary Grant, that was one of the world's best-known actors, died recently.⊗ Cary Grant, WHO was one of the world's best-known actors, died recently. (The who clause simply tells us a little more about Cary Grant.)

(3) *That* must have an antecedent (preceding noun or pronoun); in cases where there is no antecedent, we use *what* (meaning *the thing(s) that . . .*).

¿Puede decirme qué tengo que hacer?	⊗Can you tell me that to do?⊗ Can you tell me WHAT to do?
No entendí lo que dijo.	⊗I didn't understand that she said.⊗ I didn't understand WHAT she said.

The

English does not use the definite article in many cases where Spanish does.
(1) *The* is used with an uncountable or plural noun only when the meaning is specific: if the meaning is general, no article is used. Notice that the use of an adjective with a noun does not necessarily make the noun specific.

Mis bebidas preferidas son el vino y la cerveza.	⊗My favourite drinks are the wine and the beer.⊗ My favourite drinks are WINE and BEER.
No pienso volver a ese restaurante – ¡el vino era horrible!	I'm not going to that restaurant again – THE WINE was terrible!
Odio la cerveza caliente.	⊗I can't stand the warm beer.⊗ I can't stand WARM BEER. (i.e. warm beer in general.)
Lo peor de aquel 'pub' es la cerveza caliente (que venden).	The worst thing about that pub is THE WARM BEER (they sell). (i.e. specific warm beer.)

(2) Notice that in many expressions where we use *the* before, and *of* after, a noun to make it specific, we do not use *the* if we change the expression round and remove *of*.

Me encanta la música de Bach.	⊗I love the Bach's music.⊗ I love THE MUSIC OF BACH. (or: I love BACH'S MUSIC.)
La costa Oeste de Escocia es preciosa.	⊗The Scotland's West Coast is beautiful.⊗ THE WEST COAST OF SCOTLAND (or: SCOTLAND'S WEST COAST) is beautiful.

(3) Similarly, in genitive expressions with proper names.

La casa de Peter.	⊗The Peter's house.⊗ PETER'S HOUSE.
La madre de Mary.	⊗The Mary's mother.⊗ MARY'S MOTHER.

(4) There are some common words which only take *the* when we are

referring to a specific example of that word, e.g. school/church/hospital/university.

Los heridos fueron trasladados al hospital.	⊗The injured were taken to the hospital.⊗ The injured were taken TO HOSPITAL. (The idea of hospital is general, we are not thinking of a specific one.)
El nuevo hospital se inaugurará la semana que viene.	THE NEW HOSPITAL is being opened next week. (a specific hospital)

(5) *The* is only used with meals when referring to one specific meal.

Acostumbro a comer a las 2.	⊗I usually have the lunch at 2.00.⊗ I usually have LUNCH at 2.00.
La cena fue magnífica y el vino, también.	THE DINNER was superb and THE WINE too. (i.e. one specific meal)

(6) We don't normally use *the* for parts of the body when referring to a specific owner!

Se cayó y se rompió el brazo.	⊗He fell and broke the arm.⊗ He fell and broke HIS arm.
El cuerpo pesa unas 40 veces más que el cerebro.	THE BODY weighs about 40 times as much as THE BRAIN. (no specific owner)

Themselves

Themselves is the 3rd person plural reflexive pronoun; for a reciprocal action, we use *each other* (or *one another*).

Durante la cena se miraron cariñosamente (el uno al otro).	⊗They looked at themselves affectionately during the dinner.⊗ They looked at EACH OTHER affectionately during the dinner.
Salieron de la piscina y se secaron.	They got out of the pool and dried THEMSELVES.

Then

(1) *Then* is normally used in the sense of time, to say what happened next/after that, etc. To express the reason for doing something or explain why something was done, we normally use *so*, particularly when linking two parts of a sentence.

Perdí el autobús y por lo tanto tuve que ir a pie.	⊗I missed the bus, then I had to walk.⊗ I missed the bus SO I had to walk.
Terminamos la comida y luego salimos del restaurante.	We finished our meal and THEN left the restaurant.

(2) *Then* can be used when the meaning is *in that case*; it normally comes at the end of the sentence.

–Voy a Francia e Italia.	"I'm going to France and Italy."
–Entonces no necesitas visado.	"Oh, you won't need a visa, THEN."

To think

(1) For intentions, we say *to think of doing*, not with the infinitive of the following verb (except in the passive). When *think* is in the Present tense, we use the continuous form with this construction.

¿Adónde piensas ir de vacaciones el año que viene?	⊗Where do you think to go for your holidays next year?⊗
	Where ARE YOU THINKING OF GOING for your holidays next year?
Pienso jugar al tenis con Anna el próximo sábado.	⊗I think to play tennis with Anna next Saturday.⊗
	I'M THINKING OF PLAYING tennis with Anna next Saturday.
Encontraron los huesos de un animal – se creyó que pertenecían a una cebra.	⊗They found the bones of an animal – it thought it was a zebra.⊗
	They found the bones of an animal – it WAS THOUGHT TO BE a zebra.

(2) When *think* means *to have an opinion* or *to have someone in mind*, we use it with *of* or *about* – but notice the expression *I don't think much of . . .* (not *about*) (= 'no me gusta').
When the verb means *to consider something* or *to debate mentally*, we use *about*, not *of*.

–¿Qué te parece la última película de Fellini?	"What do you think OF/ABOUT Fellini's latest film?"
–No me gusta mucho.	"I don't think much OF it."
Estoy meditando su oferta muy seriamente.	⊗I'm thinking of their offer very seriously.⊗
	I'm thinking ABOUT their offer very seriously.

(3) If used with a negative idea, we normally put *think* in the negative, not the second verb.

No creo que llueva.	⊗I think it won't rain.⊗ (possible but not common.)
	I DON'T THINK IT WILL RAIN.

(4) *Think* is not used in the continuous tenses when it means *to have an opinion*.

–¿Qué te parece el nuevo jefe?	⊗"What are you thinking of the new boss?" "I am thinking he will be a success."⊗
–Creo que tendrá éxito.	"What DO YOU THINK of the new boss?"
	"I THINK he will be a success."

(5) *Think* is not used to translate an expression like 'tienes que pensar que. . .': instead, we use *remember* or *don't forget. . .*

Tienes que pensar que tus padres ya son mayores: no aguantarán un viaje tan largo.	⊗You must think that your parents are getting old: they won't be able to manage such a long journey.⊗
	You must REMEMBER that your parents are getting old: they won't be able to manage such a long journey.

This

(1) As an adjective, *this* is only used with singular nouns; the plural form is *these*.

¿Qué hace aquí toda esta gente?

⊗What are all this people doing here?⊗
What are all THESE people doing here?

(2) We say *tonight*, not *this night*.

¿Adónde vas esta noche?

⊗Where are you going this night?⊗
Where are you going TONIGHT?

Though

(1) For the difference between *though* and *in spite of/despite*, see (IN) SPITE OF.

(2) There are 2 cases when *though* can be used, but not *although*:
(a) with *even*, for emphasis.
(b) at the end of a sentence, with the meaning of *however*.

Aunque tenía mucho miedo, mantuve la calma.

⊗Even although I was frightened, I kept calm.⊗
Even THOUGH I was frightened, I kept calm.

El Concorde es fantástico, sin embargo, es muy caro.

⊗Concorde is fantastic. It's very expensive, although.⊗
Concorde is fantastic. It's very expensive, THOUGH.

Ticket See also RECEIPT

You buy a *ticket* to travel by bus/train/plane etc. or for entertainment, to go to the theatre/cinema/a sports event etc. When you buy something in a shop, you get a *receipt*.

Guárdese el ticket por si quiere cambiar el artículo.

⊗Keep your ticket in case you want to change the article.⊗
Keep your RECEIPT in case you want to change the article.

No tire el billete hasta salir del recinto del Metro.

Don't throw your TICKET away until you have left the (Underground) station.

La entrada más barata para el partido costaba 2000 pesetas.

The cheapest TICKET for the match cost £10.

Till See UNTIL

Time (1)

Time is often confused with *weather*.

–¿Lo pasaste bien?
Sí, lo pasé muy bien.

"Did you have a good time?"
⊗"Yes, it was sunny."⊗
"Yes, I ENJOYED IT/MYSELF."

–¿Tuviste buen tiempo?
Sí, hacía mucho calor.

"DID YOU HAVE GOOD WEATHER?"
"Yes, it was really hot."

Time (2)

Another time means *on another/a different occasion*; *other time* does not exist; the normal translation of 'otra vez' is *again*.

Hicisteis muy mal los deberes: tenéis que repetirlos.	⊗Your homework was terrible: you must do it another/other time.⊗
	Your homework was terrible: you must do it AGAIN.
No tenemos tiempo para terminar este ejercicio hoy: lo haremos otro día.	We haven't time to finish this exercise today: we'll do it ANOTHER TIME/ANOTHER DAY.

Times

(1) To translate 'dos veces', we say *twice*, not *two times*, e.g. *twice a week* etc.

Viaja a Paris dos veces al mes.	⊗He travels to Paris two times for/in a month.⊗
	He travels to Paris TWICE A month.

(2) Notice that we say *once or twice* but *two or three times*.

Van al teatro dos o tres veces al año.	⊗They go to the theatre twice or three times a year.⊗
	They go to the theatre TWO OR THREE times a year.

(3) With other numbers, *times* is always used.

He estado en Roma 7 o 8 veces.	I've been to Rome 7 or 8 TIMES.

Tired, tiring See ADJECTIVES (4)

To

In expressions with 'desde. . . .hasta', *to* can be used to replace *until* but it cannot be used to translate 'hasta' on its own.

Te esperaré hasta las 6.	⊗I'll wait for you to 6.00.⊗
	I'll wait for you UNTIL/TILL 6.00
Trabaja desde las 9 hasta las 5.	She works from 9 TILL/UNTIL/TO 5.

Too, too many See TOO MUCH

Too much, too many

Too much is only used before a noun (singular or uncountable).
Too many is only used before a noun (plural). Both are normal in affirmative sentences (unlike *much*).
Before an adjective or adverb, only *too* is used (or *much too. . .* for emphasis).

Hace demasiado calor para jugar al tenis.	⊗It is too much hot to play tennis.⊗
	It is (MUCH) TOO hot to play tennis. (much only for emphasis.)

Hay demasiado ruido aquí.	There IS TOO MUCH noise here.
Hay demasiada gente aquí.	There ARE TOO MANY people here.

Track See also WAY

Track translates 'pista' only in certain cases – some common ones are:

pista forestal/de montaña = track (or path)
pista de atletismo = athletics track
perder la pista de = to lose track of

But notice:

pistas de esqui = skiing slopes
pista de crucigrama/misterio etc. = a clue
pista de tenis/squash = a tennis/squash court
pista de despegue/aterrizaje = a runway

El club de tenis tiene 4 pistas nuevas.	⊗The tennis club has 4 new tracks.⊗
	The tennis club has 4 new COURTS.
El avión tuvo que esperar 20 minutos para entrar en la pista de despegue.	⊗The plane had to wait 20 minutes to get on the track.⊗
	The plane had to wait 20 minutes to get on the RUNWAY.

Transport

(1) The translation of 'subir' and 'bajar' causes problems when used with forms of transport. We say *to get on/off* a bus/train/boat etc. but *to get into/out of* a car. We don't use *to get up/down*.

Subió al autobús sin despedirse.	⊗He went/got up on the bus without saying goodbye.⊗
	He GOT ON the bus without saying goodbye.
¡Cuidado al bajar del tren!	⊗Be careful getting down from the train.⊗
	Be careful getting OFF the train.
Subió al coche y se marchó.	⊗He went into his car and drove off.⊗
	He GOT INTO his car and drove off.
Bajó del coche y caminó hacia la puerta.	⊗She got down from the car and walked towards the door.⊗
	She GOT OUT OF the car and walked towards the door.

(2) We say *to travel by car/bus/plane* etc. when we talk about a form of transport in general, but we use a different preposition if we are more specific.

Fuimos en coche.	We went BY car.
Fuimos en el coche de mi padre.	⊗We went by my father's car.⊗
	We went IN my father's car.
Viajó a Londres en tren.	He travelled to London BY train.
Viajó a Londres en el tren de las 6.30.	⊗He travelled to London by the 6.30 train.⊗
	He travelled to London ON the 6.30 train.

(To) travel see also JOURNEY

(1) *Travel* is nearly always used as a verb; as a noun, it can only mean *travel in general* and cannot be used with an article. The translation of 'un viaje' is normally *journey* or *trip*.

Es un viaje muy cansado. — ⊗It's very tiring travel.⊗
It's a very tiring JOURNEY.

Viajar es una experiencia fascinante. — ⊗The travel is a fascinating experience.⊗
TRAVEL is a fascinating experience.

(2) The plural *travels* is sometimes used for either a very long trip or a succession of trips.

–Así que, ¿ya te vas otra vez de viaje? — "So, you're off on your TRAVELS again, are you?"

Trip See JOURNEY

True

True is an adjective; the noun is *(the) truth*.

¡Te lo juro, es verdad! — ⊗Really, is true/it's the true!⊗
Really, IT'S TRUE!

Mis padres me enseñaron a decir siempre la verdad. — ⊗My parents taught me always to tell the true.⊗
My parents taught me always to tell the TRUTH.

U

Unique

In English, *unique* means *the only one of its kind, there is no other like it*. The translation of 'único' meaning *not more than one* is *only*.

Era la única persona que había allí. — ⊗He was the unique person there.⊗
He was the ONLY person there.

Su manera de pintar es única. — His style of painting is UNIQUE.

Venecia es una ciudad única. — Venice is a UNIQUE city.

Unless

Unless can often replace *if. . .not*, but not in a sentence where the first part is the result of the second part not happening. A good "rule" is to use *unless* only in cases where Spanish uses 'a menos que'.

Estaría más contento si no tuviera que pagar tantos impuestos. — ⊗I'd be happier unless I had to pay so much tax.⊗
I'd be happier IF I DIDN'T HAVE to pay so much tax.

Estaría mejor si no llevara el pelo tan largo.

⊗He'd look better unless he wore his hair so long.⊗

He'd look better IF HE DIDN'T WEAR his hair so long.

Se tarda una hora en llegar, a menos que haya mucho tráfico.

It takes an hour to get there, IF the traffic ISN'T heavy (or: UNLESS the traffic IS heavy).

Until

Until is only used in expressions of time. To translate 'hasta' in expressions of physical distance, we normally use *as far as*; and with numbers, *up to*.

Trabajo hasta las 9 cada noche.

I work UNTIL 9.00 every night.

Sube por esta calle hasta el semáforo y luego gira a la izquierda.

⊗Go up this street until the traffic-lights and then turn left.⊗

Go up this street AS FAR AS the traffic-lights and then turn left.

Había hasta 50 personas en la fiesta.

⊗There were until 50 people at the party.⊗

There were UP TO 50 people at the party.

Used to

Used to. . ., preceded by a subject only, and followed by a verb in the infinitive form, refers to a past situation which is no longer true. (= 'solía ser/hacer').
To be used to. . ., followed by a noun, or a verb in the gerund form, means 'to be accustomed to', often with the idea of initial difficulty.
Usually (= *normally*) is an adverb of frequency which indicates a habitual action, whether in the Present or in the Past.

Antes vivía en Londres pero ahora vivo en Birmingham.

⊗I was used to live/I used live in London, but now I live in Birmingham.⊗

I USED TO LIVE in London, but now I live in Birmingham.

Al principio me era muy difícil levantarme a las 6, pero ahora me he acostumbrado.

⊗At first I found it difficult, but now I am used to get up at 6.00.⊗

At first I found it difficult, but now I AM USED TO GETTING UP at 6.00.

Cuando vine a Barcelona por primera vez, la encontré muy ruidosa, pero me he acostumbrado ya.

⊗When I first came to Barcelona, I found it very noisy, but now I am used.⊗

When I first came to Barcelona, I found it very noisy, but now I AM USED TO IT.

Acostumbro a ir/Normalmente voy al cine una vez por semana.

⊗I use/used to go to the cinema once a week.⊗

I USUALLY GO to the cinema once a week.

Usually

See USED TO

V

Very

(1) *Very* is used with adjectives or adverbs – it is not an expression of quantity.

Había mucha gente en la fiesta.	⊗There were very people at the party.⊗ There were A LOT OF people at the party.

(2) It is not used with comparatives, or with adjectives of extremes, which do not need to be reinforced, e.g. *fantastic*, *superb*, *dreadful*, *beautiful*, *disgusting*.

El chino es mucho más difícil de aprender que el inglés.	⊗Chinese is very more difficult to learn than English.⊗ Chinese is MUCH more difficult to learn than English.
Lo pasamos realmente bien.	⊗We had a very fantastic time.⊗ We had a FANTASTIC time.

(3) It is often wrongly used instead of *too* with an adjective.

Estaba demasiado cansado para estudiar más.	⊗He was very tired to study any more.⊗ He was TOO tired to study any more.

Voyage

A *voyage* is a journey made by sea: in other contexts, we use *journey* or *trip*.

El viaje en tren fue lento y aburrido.	⊗The voyage by train was slow and boring.⊗ The JOURNEY by train was slow and boring.
El viaje en barco duró 4 horas.	The VOYAGE lasted 4 hours.

W

To wait

(1) See TO EXPECT.
(2) When *to wait* is used with a direct object, *for* must precede the object.

Te esperaré después de clase.	⊗I'll wait you after class.⊗ I'll WAIT FOR you after class.
Esperaba el tren.	⊗He was waiting the train.⊗ He was WAITING FOR the train.

To want

(1) *To want* must be followed by *to* when preceding another verb.

Quiero viajar por (toda) Europa. — ⊗I want travel round Europe.⊗
I WANT TO travel round Europe.

(2) It is followed by an object and infinitive when 2 different subjects are involved.

¿Quieres que te ayude? — ⊗Do you want that I help you?⊗
Do you WANT ME TO HELP you?

(3) *To want to say* means 'tener ganas de decir'; we use *to mean* to translate 'querer decir' in the sense of 'significar' (see TO MEAN).

No te entiendo – ¿qué quieres decir? — ⊗I don't understand you – what do you want to say?⊗
I don't understand you – what do you MEAN?

No tengo ganas de decir nada por ahora. — I don't WANT TO SAY anything at the moment.

Warm See HOT

To watch

To watch is similar to *to look at* but it is normally used for a spectacle of some sort, i.e. there must be movement. *To watch* a person means more than just *to look at* them: you follow their movements, gestures etc.

Miró la tarjeta con atención. — ⊗He watched the card carefully.⊗
He LOOKED AT the card carefully.

¿Viste aquel programa anoche? — Did you WATCH that programme last night?

Fue vigilado por detectives durante dos semanas. — He was WATCHED by detectives for two weeks.

Way

(1) *Way* means *how to go to a place*, *route* ('recorrido'). It is not used when indicating a specific 'camino' or 'pista' – for this, we say *path* or *track*.

¿Sabes ir a Oxford? — Do you know the WAY to Oxford?

Hay un pequeño camino que lleva a la cima (de la montaña). — ⊗There is a small way that leads to the top (of the mountain).⊗
There is a small PATH that leads to the top (of the mountain).

No te puedes perder – sólo tienes que seguir el camino. — You can't lose your WAY – just follow the PATH/TRACK.

(2) We say *on the way to a place*, not *in*. *In the way* means someone or something is preventing you from going where you want to go.

–¿La Garriga? Sí, está camino de Vic.	⊗"La Garriga? Yes, it's in the way to Vic."⊗
	"La Garriga? Yes, it's ON the way to Vic."
¿Puedes apartarte, por favor? Me estás tapando/No me dejas pasar.	Could you move, please? You're IN my way.

To wear

See TO CARRY, TO DRESS

Well

See also ADVERBS

Well is the adverb derived from the adjective *good*, with which it is often confused. *Well* is only used as an adjective when talking about health.

Juegas bien al ajedrez.	⊗You play chess very good.⊗
	You play chess very WELL.
–¿Qué tal la película?	"What's the film like?"
–Está bien/Es buena.	⊗"It's very well."⊗
	"It's very GOOD."
–¿Cómo estás?	"How are you?"
–(Muy) bien, gracias.	⊗"I'm good, thanks."⊗
	"I'm (very) WELL, thanks."

Notice the difference, and order of words, in the following:

Habla muy bien el inglés.	⊗He speaks very well English.⊗
	He speaks very GOOD English.
	or: He speaks English very WELL.

What

See THAT

What?

See also WHO?

When *What*? is the subject of a verb, the auxiliary verb *do/did* is not used.

–¿Qué pasó?	⊗What did happen?⊗
	What HAPPENED?
–¿Qué es lo que le motiva?	⊗What does motivate him?⊗
	What MOTIVATES him?

Compare a sentence where *What*? is the object of the verb:

¿Qué hicisteis durante las vacaciones?	What DID YOU DO in the holidays?

When

In time clauses, *when* is followed by a Present or Present Perfect tense, even though the meaning is future.

Empezaremos la reunión cuando él venga.	⊗We'll start the meeting when he will arrive.⊗
	We'll start the meeting when he ARRIVES. (or: HAS ARRIVED.)

Which

(1) *Whose*, not *which*, is used as a relative possessive word.

Ése es el hombre cuya casa visitamos. ⊗That's the man which house we visited.⊗

That's the man WHOSE house we visited.

(2) *Of which* can be used when referring to things, but not people. Notice also the different word order.

Escribió dos novelas, cuyos títulos no recuerdo. She wrote two novels, WHOSE TITLES (or: THE TITLES OF WHICH) I can't remember.

Who See THAT

Who?

As with *What*?, *Who*? does not take *do/did* when it is the subject of the verb.

¿Quién te lo dijo? ⊗Who did tell you?⊗

Who TOLD you?

¿Quién te da clases? ⊗Who does give you classes?⊗

Who GIVES you classes?

¿A quién viste ayer? Who DID you see yesterday?

(The) whole

Whole (meaning 'todo' or 'entero') often has a similar meaning to *all (the)* but it cannot be used: (a) with uncountable nouns and (b) with a singular noun when there is no determiner before it (e.g. the, this, our etc.).

Robó todo el dinero y se escapó. ⊗He stole the whole money and ran away.⊗

He stole ALL THE money and ran away.

Me gustaría visitar toda la ciudad/la ciudad entera. ⊗I would like to visit whole city.⊗

I would like to visit THE WHOLE city. (or: ALL THE city)

To win

A player or team can *win* a trophy/title/championship/match/cup etc. but not an opponent/a rival/the other team etc.; in these cases, we use *to beat*. You can *win* money in a lottery/in a competition/on the football pools etc. but when you work, you *earn* money.

Becker venció a McEnroe en la final. ⊗Becker won McEnroe in the final.⊗

Becker BEAT McEnroe in the final.

El Everton ganó la Recopa en 1985: venció al Rapid de Viena por 3 a 1. Everton WON the Cup-winners' Cup in 1985: they BEAT Rapid Vienna 3–1.

¿Cuánto gana al mes? — ⊗How much does he win a month?⊗
How much does he EARN a month?

Ganó 2 millones de pesetas en la lotería. — She WON two million pesetas in the lottery.

To wish

Using the correct tense in *wish* constructions often causes problems.
(1) *Wish* is only followed by *would* with the sense of complaining about someone's habits, or to insist on something. It is never followed by the future.

A ver si dejas de quejarte. — I wish you WOULD STOP complaining.
¡Si por lo menos no hiciera tanto ruido! — I wish he WOULDN'T MAKE so much noise!
Espero que mañana haga sol. — ⊗I wish it would/will be sunny tomorrow.⊗
I HOPE it will be sunny tomorrow.

(2) If the *wish* is about a situation in the present, the following verb will be in the past.

Ojalá fuese rico. — ⊗I wish I would be rich.⊗
I wish I WAS rich.

(3) If the *wish* is about a situation in the past, the following verb will be in the Past Perfect.

Ojalá me hubiera escrito. — ⊗I wish she would have written to me.⊗
I wish she HAD WRITTEN to me.

Without

When *without* is followed by a verb, we must use the '-ing' form, not the infinitive.

Salió sin cerrar la puerta. — ⊗He walked out without (to) close the door.⊗
He walked out without CLOSING the door.

Word order

The following are the most common problems of Word Order.
(1) Reported Questions – see REPORTED QUESTIONS.
(2) Adverbs of frequency.
The position of adverbs like usually, sometimes, often, never, always, etc. is normally: (a) after the verb *to be*; (b) before any other principal verb; (c) when two auxiliary verbs are used, before the second one.

Vamos al cine a menudo. — ⊗We go often to the cinema.⊗
We OFTEN GO to the cinema.

¡Siempre llega tarde! — ⊗He always is late!⊗
He IS ALWAYS late!

Nunca hubiese aprobado el examen sin su ayuda.	⊗He would have never passed the exam without her help.⊗
	He WOULD NEVER HAVE passed the exam without her help.

(3) With Neither/Nor and so – see NEITHER/NOR and SO.
(4) With the verbs *to like* and *to enjoy* – see TO LIKE and TO ENJOY.
(5) Incorrect inversion of subject and verb – where a literal translation from the Spanish would place a verb or adjective before the subject, which is possible only in certain cases in English.

Su nueva novela es muy interesante.	⊗Is/It's very interesting her new novel.⊗
	HER NEW NOVEL IS VERY INTERESTING.

Work

The noun *work* is only countable when it has the meaning of e.g. *a work of art*, *a work of charity* etc. To translate 'un trabajo', we have to say *a job*.

Estoy buscando un nuevo trabajo.	⊗I'm looking for a new work.⊗
	I'm looking for a new JOB.
Me gusta mucho mi trabajo.	I really enjoy my WORK/JOB.
¡Las obras de Dali son tan originales!	Dali's WORKS are so original!

To work

We say *to work for* a firm, company, etc.; *to work in* a shop/an office/a factory etc.

Trabaja en ICI.	⊗He works in ICI.⊗
	He works FOR ICI.
Trabaja en una tienda de ropa.	He works IN a clothes shop.

To worry

We say *to worry about* something, not *for* something.

Estoy muy preocupado por este problema.	⊗I am very worried for this problem.⊗
	I am very worried ABOUT this problem.

Worth

Worth is used with the verb *to be* to express (a) the value of something and (b) if an action is *worth the trouble* ('vale la pena'). With this second meaning, the following verb must be in the '–ing' form, not the infinitive.

Esa casa vale una fortuna.	That house IS WORTH a fortune.
No vale la pena ver esa película.	⊗It is not worth to see that film.⊗
	It is not WORTH SEEING that film. (or: That film is not WORTH SEEING.)

To wound

See TO DAMAGE

Y

Yesterday

We say *yesterday morning/afternoon/evening* (without a preposition) but *last night*.

¿Qué hiciste ayer por la mañana/tarde?	⊗What did you do yesterday in the morning/afternoon?⊗ What did you do YESTERDAY MORNING/AFTERNOON?
¿Adónde fuiste anoche?	⊗Where did you go yesterday night?⊗ Where did you go LAST NIGHT?

Yet

See ALREADY, STILL

Indice